"Failing at an early age produces character, determination, and humility, all of which can never be learned without it. If you do fail, however, it means you had the courage to take a risk, which, in itself, is quite admirable."

— CHAPTER 1

"Failing should be thought of like a photograph. You see it, but only for the instant in which the image was captured. Photography can be misleading, just like failing."

— CHAPTER 1

"Failing is not failure; how you react to your failure is the indication of whether you have truly failed or not."

— CHAPTER 1

"Courage often is a result of failure in the same way that success is a result of courage; therefore, to achieve success in life, you have to overcome failure with courage."

— CHAPTER 1

"The only way to be found is to admit we are lost."

— CHAPTER 2

Worry in itself is not a bad thing; we need to be careful of what we are ultimately worrying about, however. You want to have your worries to be in parallel with the Lord—not in parallel with the worries of man.

"We all hope; it is what we hope for that demonstrates where our true heart is. All the criminal hoped for is to be found again; in his repentance and in his character, that happened."

"With Christianity, the less you are in control, the more you are in control."

"The nice thing about knowing that Jesus died for our sins is that once we know that simple truth, our lives are transformed. Sin in no longer chasing us; we know longer have to dodge and weave to hide; we are free, but only if we admit our sin."

"Admitting your blind spot is a challenging thing to, but it produces a realness is relationships, because it shows the person you know that you are only human. That humbleness opens the door for them to be humble back to you, opening the way for a deeper form of communication than you thought was possible."

"I often find myself trying to be perfect, and when I'm not, I find myself trying to cover up my sin when I should be doing the opposite because Christ died for me."

"The last thing I like to do is admit that I am wrong, but when I do, I know God is smiling; after all, it means my complete trust is in him."

– CHAPTER 3

"To God however, beauty means admitting we are broken and lost, needing to pick up God's rhythms to regain it. Whatever we do is not enough because we have all fallen short, so very short of his Glory. Only in the cross, can we regain that beauty."

– CHAPTER 3

"The opposite of sarcasm is vulnerability. You can tell when a man is strong when he is more attuned to the latter rather than the former."

– CHAPTER 3

"Without integrity, a person is empty. The emptiness comes from that person's lack of respect for reality; in life, reality accounts for everything that is worthwhile."

– CHAPTER 4

"To make a difference, we have to make a change. The reason for this is rather simple: we are all fallen—in need of his saving grace."

– CHAPTER 4

"It is only when we hide our sin that we get into trouble. Admitting your trouble is the surest way to get out of trouble in Christianity."

– CHAPTER 4

"Being honest doesn't require you to be good-looking, smart, or clever, it only requires showing your authentic self to the world. Chances are, if you are honest, people will appreciate you more, listen to you more, and value you more. The reason for this is simple: you will now be set apart in a rare class."

— CHAPTER 4

"To take it learning even further, one has to learn from anybody and everybody, even the flawed. In doing so, your life will be changed, and once your life is changed, you will change others."

— CHAPTER 5

"Only when we admit that we are less, and He is more, will we be found. The reason for this simple: admitting that we are less doesn't make us less, it makes us more."

— CHAPTER 5

"With power, often comes pride. That pride is not from above, but down below. The only thing we need to be prideful of is what Jesus did for us on the cross. It was the opposite of prideful. Because of this, it was definition of powerful."

— CHAPTER 5

"Jesus never seeks earthly might. To be a king is to be rich, powerful, carry a good name, and have lots of servants. I guess Jesus never got the memo. For him, power was in being *with* us, not *over* us."

— CHAPTER 5

"Most people are too proud to learn, but the most impactful of people always take the position that in order to impact people, you can never learn enough."

– CHAPTER 5

"We're blessed in that when Jesus said, 'It is finished', what it meant for us is that it was only getting started. Through his death on the cross, we could start to love again, start to matter again, but most of all, we could start to heal again. In healing again, we can start to live again. And we are doubly blessed in that most leaders close their doors. Most famous people try to avoid the paparazzi and fans. Not Jesus though. He told us he would be with us until the end of the age."

– CHAPTER 5

"We are all fake, all lost, void of anything worthwhile without the blood of Jesus. We all need blood in order to survive. Why live only to survive, why not live to thrive? We can, but only with the blood of Jesus. Only his blood is pure, that is for certain."

– CHAPTER 6

"When we repent, we are secure. It's a security that is much more comforting than a 401K or a seatbelt in a car. It's a security that transcends all understanding, and once you have it, all you want to do is pass it on. After all, to give that security is to give life. And it's not just life on this earth, it's life everlasting."

– CHAPTER 6

"I need Jesus' blood just as I need oxygen, food, water, and shelter. Without it, I can never survive, never thrive. Without it I am a nobody, I can achieve nothing. With it, I am not only powerful, I am free."

– CHAPTER 6

"We're often taught to present our best selves to the world even though deep down we know this is not for the best."

– CHAPTER 6

"You can tell how much someone believes in the cross by how open they are about their own sin."

– CHAPTER 6

"Thankfulness shouldn't be situation-based because difficult times have a way of shaping us in a stronger, more effective way than a seemingly encouraging time. It's more challenging to grow when things are going well. When you're at the very bottom, upward is the only direction you can go."

– CHAPTER 8

"To be thankful isn't to walk around with a smile on your face all the time. Jesus didn't have a smile on his face when he was crucified. After all, didn't he cry out, "why have you forsaken me?" He did have the wherewithal to trust God during that time, however. When you trust in God during the toughest of times, He credits that as thankfulness."

– CHAPTER 8

"For me, gratitude can frame meaningless drudgery into meaningful opportunities."

– CHAPTER 8

"Disciple is the root word of discipline. So why is discipline seen as an extremely *negative* word and disciple as an extremely *positive* word?"

– CHAPTER 9

"It might seem like a paradox, but you want to try to be a person that no one wants to be around because when he leaves your presence they are immediately disappointed by the decreased level of character and encouragement they are now forced to be around in terms of dealing with other people."

– CHAPTER 9

"I challenge the people I respect, but to those who I have neither the capacity nor ability to change, I am silent."

– CHAPTER 9

"The criminal serves as a guide to us all. He's humble, yet unafraid, clever, without the usual pretentiousness; but most of all, he is loyal, and, in his loyalty, he became the first convert to Christianity; in doing so, he joined Jesus in paradise forever."

– CONCLUSION

THE CRIMINAL

THE POWER OF AN APOLOGY

THOMAS FELLOWS

THE CRIMINAL
THE POWER OF AN APOLOGY

© 2020 Thomas Fellows

ISBN 978-1-947773-67-7 paperback
978-1-947773-68-7 eBook

Yawn's Publishing
678-880-1922
www.yawnspublishing.com

www.yawnspublishing.com
678-880-1922
Canton, Georgia

First Edition 2020

Cover design by Easty Lambert-Brown

Printed in the United States of America

CONTENTS

ACKNOLWEDGEMENTS

I want to thank Lindsay Shelton who could teach us all a thing or two about character.

I want to thank Katie Jones, who was the first person to tell me I should write a book.

I want thank Vic Pentz, former Senior Pastor of Peachtree Presbyterian Church. There was a young man in your pews in the early 2000's who was listening and absorbing every word you said. That young man was me.

I want to thank Kendall Person for giving me the idea for the title of the book.

I want to thank Ryan Akers of Campus Outreach. He was instrumental in my faith progression in college at Samford.

I want to thank the following History and English teachers at Westminster who have already been thanked in my previous book, *Forget Self Help*. They are Tiffany Boozer, Thad Persons, Joe Tribble, and Jennifer Dracos. They have been the lifeblood of my writing/career endeavors over the last eleven years.

I want to say thanks to Bubba Chrismer who told me some of the wisest words I've ever heard 12 years ago: "you've heard the saying, you are what you eat; instead, I say, you are what you read."

I want to say thanks to Jessica Williams, my 8th grade English Workshop teacher. It was in her class where I developed the ability to look at music (specifically, "One Sweet World" by Dave Matthews) the same way we look at writing. Although I did have a crush on you, I didn't go to your extra-help for that reason; I went to work on my writing.

INTRODUCTION

How one person in the Bible who could have such a great impact on me is pretty apparent if you've ever gotten the chance to know me. I'm rather obsessed with studying character. Does that mean I myself display great character? No, not at all. Well, at times I do, but at other times I definitely don't. But, do I see things that other people simply don't see in others? Why, yes, I do believe that, absolutely. That's why I wrote *Forget Self-Help*, and that's why I wrote *The Criminal: The Power of An Apology*. Is it contradictory that I am a Christian and obsessed with character? Unfortunately, I believe this could be the case.

Take an example that happened recently from my own life in Atlanta. The exact same situation ironically is highlighted in *Blink* by Malcom Gladwell. I am having lunch on the storied patio at one of the most classic restaurants in the South, Horseradish Grill: no tourists, only locals, just the way I like it. It's with Alex Kaufman, a friend of mine who also graduated from The Westminster Schools in Atlanta, GA. He's older but has never really treated me like that. He's smart; he went to Hamilton for college and Emory for law school. And he's ambitious; he's running for a congressional seat in his early 30's. I'm not including him in this book because of any of that, I'm including him because in just a split second of time, he reiterated why I thought he had great character, similar character to

14

the criminal on the cross. I realized this because of one simple act: a waiter accidentally drops a fork and almost instantaneously Kaufman reaches to get it. It re-iterated my view of Kaufman's character because he did the something similar the last time I saw him at an accounting Christmas party a few months before. As soon as I started telling him about the book and how to purchase it, he whips out his phone and buys it on Amazon. And, when we met up, he told me that he had read it as well.

In this book, I speak to many character traits that the criminal on the cross possessed. They are humility, integrity, courage, gratitude, discipline, and vulnerability. All of those traits link together to achieve grace. They are all action traits.

I have had discussions with pastors before about whether it is okay to try to strive for being "a man after God's own heart." From discussions with some pastors, I feel they almost look at this as sinful; I make the claim that it is not only not sinful, but also an important part of living out the Christian life and even more so gives us a better avenue to live out the Great Commission of Matthew 28:19-20. In order for the criminal on the cross to be the first convert to Christianity, he had to take *action* to achieve grace from Jesus' blood. Part of this action was to display the character traits just I mentioned.

It is not easy to display these characteristics and if you know me in real life, you're probably wondering why me of all people is commenting on them because I struggle to live them out on a daily basis. Sometimes the best person to teach you what to do often is a person that struggles with these issues themselves. For example, if you are trying to get rid of a slice in golf, it can be advantageous to learn how to combat this problem with someone who struggles with it.

They often know the ins and outs of the problem and what causes it more so than anyone else.

My hope is that you will not only learn something from the book, but you will also be entertained. Other than the Bible, I use classic works of literature, historical figures, movies, and music to stress and illustrate my points.

Malcom Gladwell once said, "good writing does not succeed or fail on the strength of its ability to persuade. It succeeds or fails on the strength of its ability to engage you, to make you think, to give you a glimpse into someone else's head." I hope I achieved this throughout the pages of *The Criminal.*

"It's amazing the way things, apparently disconnected, hang together." – CHARLIE, *FLOWERS FOR ALGERNON*, DANIEL KEYES

"Everyone has a moment in history which belongs particularly to him. It is the moment when his emotions achieve their most powerful sway over him, and afterward when you say to this person 'the world today' or 'life' or 'reality' he will assume that you mean this moment, even if it is fifty years past. The world, through his unleashed emotions, imprinted itself upon him, and he carries the stamp of that passing moment forever." – *A SEPARATE PEACE*, JOHN KNOWLES

"Between my finger and my thumb
The squat pen rests.
I'll dig with it."
– "DIGGING" by Seamus Heaney

"If conversion to Christianity makes no improvement in a man's outward actions – if he continues to be just a snobbish or spiteful or envious or ambitious as he was before – then I think we must suspect that his 'conversion' was largely imaginary; and after one's original conversion, every time one thinks one has made an advance, that is the test to apply. Fine feelings, new insights, greater interest in 'religion' mean nothing unless they make our actual behavior better; just as in an illness 'feeling better' is not much good if the thermometer shows that your temperature is still going up. In that sense the outer world is quite right to judge Christianity by its results. Christ told us to judge by results. A tree is known by its fruit; or, as we say, the proof of the pudding is in the eating. When we Christians behave badly, or fail to behave well, we are making Christianity unbelievable to the outside world. The war-time posters told us that Careless Talk costs Lives. It is equally true that Careless Lives cost Talk. Our careless lives set the outer world taking; and we give them grounds for talking in a way that throws doubt on the truth of Christianity itself." – C.S. LEWIS

"Most people have a hard time admitting error, apologizing, changing our minds. It takes more than a typical amount of self-awareness to realize that one is wrong and to admit it." – NASSIR GHAEMI, *A FIRST RATE MADNESS: UNCOVERING THE LINKS BETWEEN LEADERSHIP AND MENTAL ILLNESS*

Another one ...

1

Courage That Comes from Failure

It is often said that character is what you truly are when no one is watching you. While that may be true, how much more important is it to show character when people are watching you? Exponentially speaking, it is much more important because your actions will be seen and copied by many around you in the present and in the age to come. This book is about a character in the Bible who is so obscure that he does not have a name. He is just known as "the criminal." This book is written from a Christian angle but is meant to be read by people of all faiths.

Just like my previous book, *Forget Self-Help: Re-Examining the Golden Rule*, I argue throughout that Christians often struggle with displaying character, and, from my perspective, many pastors argue it is almost a sin to have a conscience—something that I believe God is shuddering at exactly how this thought got into Christianity. Luckily, I think God put the criminal next to Jesus right before he dies as a reminder of how to be a people of great character.

Don't get me wrong, I think that Jesus is the Author and Perfecter of our faith. At the same time, however, shouldn't we as Christians be known by people of other faiths as a people that can be counted on? Wouldn't Christianity spread faster if that were the case? Below shows the passage in Luke 23:40-43 which we will examine throughout this book.

But the other criminal rebuked him. "Don't you fear God," he said, "since you are under the same sentence? We are punished justly, for we are getting what our deeds deserve. But this man has done nothing wrong." Then he said, "Jesus, remember me when you come into your kingdom. Jesus answered him, "Truly I tell you, today you will be with me in paradise."

The thing that sets the criminal apart from other people is that he actually possesses enough of a conscience to admit that he was the one who had fallen short. Admitting you are wrong to others and to God is the first step to a powerful relationship with both your fellow man and God. The times I have respected someone the most has been when they have had the empathy to step into my shoes and simply declare that they had messed up. It is even more impressive when they do this without any prodding. It's certainly rare, but most things that are worth something in life are.

Jesus certainly agrees with this last statement; that's why he tells him, "truly I tell you, today you will be with me in paradise." Jesus is reiterating the fact that we do not, indeed, possess the power to get into heaven through our own good works, but are in need of his saving grace. Jesus knew how much we depend on ourselves for our self-worth when it is really Him who is all we need. At the same point, however, it requires some action on our part by admitting that we are wrong.

In this book, I'll take you through the importance of admitting your faults and realizing the power you have over yourself when you do, in fact, have the courage to admit you are wrong. It's difficult at first, but later on produces a power in you that is unable to be stopped—enabling your relationship with The Lord and others to thrive.

*

Failing at an early age produces character, determination, and humility, all of which can never be learned without it. If you do fail, however, it means you had the courage to take a risk, which is in itself, quite admirable. I can vividly remember my History teacher in 10th grade disagreeing with our school's mission statement because it included the words well-rounded in them. He told us do you want to simply be a jack of all trades, or a master of one? He told us that too many kids at the school were afraid of failing—were afraid of sticking their head out and trying to be something special. He said that you could easily fit into the crowd by being average at many things, but if you tried to be good at one thing and failed, you would risk being called a failure.

In the same vein, J.K. Rowling said something profound at a Harvard Commencement Speech: "It is impossible to live without failing at something, unless you live so cautiously that you might as well not have lived at all—in which case, you fail by default. The knowledge that you have emerged wiser and stronger from setbacks means that you are, ever after, secure in your ability to survive. You will never truly know yourself, or the strength of your relationships, until both have been tested by adversity. Such knowledge is a true gift, for all that it is painfully won, and it has been worth more than any qualification I ever earned."

I've learned in my own life, that one's response to failure is the truest barometer for success, not necessarily one's own talents they possess in the first place. I've learned that most people are too fragile to try something great because they are afraid to fail. That's what

Rowling speaks to when she warns people, "that living too cautiously means that you have not lived at all." From a Christian perspective, it's an absolute insult not to better your fellow man and live for His glory. True, there may be risk involved, but when you are doing what Gold called you to do with the talent he bestows among you, your risk diminishes.

One of my friends from growing up in Atlanta, Warren Coleman, was telling me a phrase his kids would repeat called "try hard" when someone on the baseball team that he coached would put substantial effort into a play. It killed me when I heard this. Cynicism and sarcasm have replaced everything good in this world.

In "Learning to Allow temporary failure: potential benefits, supportive practices and teacher concern" by Orit Alfi, Idit Katz, and Avi Assor, they bring up many valid arguments and points as to while it is not only okay for someone to fail, but necessary in their development and a precursor to their future success. All three authors of the paper talked to many teachers during a workshop that dealt with potential failure. The teachers intentionally set up tasks for the students where they would not fail. The article goes on to say that, 'when we discussed this issue with the teachers, we realized that they clearly preferred to assign pupils tasks that are certain of success ... teachers appeared to hold an underlying belief that even temporary and minor experiences of failure cause severe harm to pupils' perceived and actual competence.'" This sort of thinking robs a child of the ability to get back on their feet when they go through hard times. Going through the most harrowing of times has made me that much more thankful than for the easy times. The criminal sinning was certainly a precursor for his becoming one of the most successful characters in the whole Bible. Rising from failure is far more impressive than being successful in the first place.

Sometimes when you fail, as Kanye West insinuates in "Gold-Digger," you have to do the dirty work. What that means takes courage, but if you succeed, there's glory in the end. Rolling up your sleeves takes risk, too. After all, it is easier to stand on the sideline than to put yourself into the game. First Lady Rosalyn Carter said it best when she remarked, "You must accept that you might fail; then, if you do your best and still don't win, at least you can be satisfied that you've tried. If you don't accept failure as a possibility, you don't set high goals, you don't branch out, you don't try - you don't take the risk." Most of the people I have met in life have not taken that risk—have not branched out as First Lady Carter said. Who would we be as a nation if we hadn't had strong leaders in the past who have dared to be great? You owe it not just to yourself to try to be a star, but to others. Once you lead, others will surely follow you.

One of my favorite role-models of all time, Martin Luther King Jr., once said, "The ultimate measure of a man is not where he stands in moments of comfort and convenience, but where he stands at times of challenge and controversy." The reason why this quote rings true is most are tempted to just give up when they are challenged. The reason for this is simple: it is safe; it does not require risk. A pledge brother in of mine in college had gotten in a horrific accident at the lake after he had attempted to do a flip. He landed poorly and should have died that day. But he didn't. After months and months of rehab, he began to walk, slowly, but surely. His whole situation made me think about an interview question that is rarely asked in the jobs I had been interviewing before I got my job at Walmart. The question is what have you overcome in your life that makes you confident that when you face trouble in this specific job, you will be able to overcome the challenge and ultimately be victorious? Is asking what someone has achieved really a fair question? Sure, I received national media coverage for my first book, but look at the advantage I had. All four of my teachers I mentioned in my acknowledgment section held degrees from Ivy league schools or near Ivy League. In baseball terminology, I was already rounding third with full steam behind me headed for home. The measure of a leader is not what he has achieved, but what he has overcome. Achievement is deceptive; you can achieve without having to ever overcome anything. But, when you overcome something, achievement is inevitable and more permanent.

Furthermore, as Malcom Gladwell writes in his *New York Times* Bestseller, *David and Goliath*, there are so many positive things that come from failing. Many things can happen when adversity comes upon an individual. They can die from the blow, they can be scared the rest of their life from the blow, or they can grow stronger from what happened. Gladwell speaks of a person growing stronger from the blow when he uses General McCurdy writes about being in the London Blitz in World War 1. He writes,

We are all of us not merely liable to fear, we are also prone to be afraid of being afraid, and the conquering of fear produces exhilaration ... when we have been afraid that we may panic in an air raid, and, when it has happened, we have exhibited to others nothing but a calm exterior and we are now safe, the contrast between the previous apprehension and the present relief and feeling of security promotes a self-confidence that is the very father and mother of courage.

Above, what these teachers are doing is not helping them out, it's actually robbing the child's ability to live in a realistic life. We are all going to fail at some point, we are all going to be put in times that strain us in some way, so why would these teachers try to keep those kids from experiencing that from an early age? If anything, if they do learn how to fail, they will be more prepared to deal with it if they have gone through tough times in the first place. After all, Michael Jordan once said, "I've failed over and over and over again in my life and that is why I succeed."[1]

When the authors of the previously mentioned article asked a teacher why they were so weary of allowing a student to temporarily fail, that teacher said: "my pupils experience enough frustrations in their natural environment … I wouldn't like to discourage them … I want school to be a corrective experience for them." Teachers who employ these tactics are not helping their students; they are actually hurting them. To struggle is not to grow weaker, it actually makes us grow stronger. When instructing, leading, and teaching the next generation, we must remember this. The criminal didn't go through a "quick fix" and neither can our next generation. Pain and frustration go hand in hand with achievement and success. Without the former, there is no way to have the latter.

Sometimes, we have to get to the place where Ariana Grande speaks of when we she said that she "Ain't got no tears left to cry." Sometimes, we do have to hit rock bottom. For me, this occurred in the spring of 2018 when I had an interaction with someone who was more of an acquaintance in high school, but now is a good friend of mine. His name is Smith Haverty. We were supposed to have met for coffee twice, and I stood him up *twice*. The second time it happened, I could tell it had—rightfully so—made him pretty angry. He certainly let me know he was angry. I not only

---

[1] Written by Jamie Barrett for a Nike TV commercial in 1997.

deserved it; I needed it. During the past few years I had become quite lethargic, would miss scheduled meetings, and flights for work all of the time.[2] I had also gained 30 pounds because I slept in until 10:00 or so the majority of days. In short, I had hit rock bottom.

Having Smith by my side to help me out through the next few weeks and months were paramount to me starting to turn back into myself. Until that moment, I had become a shadow of my current self. That's exactly what sin does to us: it makes us become a shadow of our former selves. Smith was there for me during that time. He would text me to wake up in the morning, offer to look over my resume; in short, he did what Christ does for us when we admit our sin. I had to take *action* in order for this to happen. I had to admit I had a problem and needed help. In many ways, I had to be humble and honest, two of the qualities that I talk about in the book. Sometimes a helping hand is all we need. I found that in Smith, just as we can also find that in Christ.

In what has been one of the most successful songs of all time, "Try Again," by Aaliyah, she promotes a simple message about getting through hard times and coming out on top in the end. It is simple in the sense that she consistently belts out the lyrics, "If you fail at first, get back up and be brave in your next attempt." Anyone that has gotten themselves out of a hole can easily see that getting yourself out of the hole cannot only be complex, but a challenge. There is no time where I demonstrated this more than when during my early career in software sales. I'll never forget. I was calling on a CRM[3] campaign for my first campaign and was failing miserably at

---

[2] There was actually a flight to San Diego that I was six hours late to.
[3] Customer Relationship Management software that helps companies keep track of customers and prospects

it. It didn't help that it was a near impossible campaign, but it also didn't help that my selling tactics were tepid. At one point, my manager, urged me to instead of just hanging up after a prospect would say no, to instead try to stay on the phone a bit longer to see if they would say yes to another call. The manager led me the way any leader should lead someone: always from the side, never from behind.

The stronger reason my luck changed from failing into success was because of the help of my brother, Chris. Chris made average grades at Westminster—which is impressive in its own right. He had a 3.75 at UGA, and would go on to get his CFA, then matriculate into Goizueta Emory Business school, where he would be honored with being named the Orator at graduation. His intelligence was needed during that time. He taught me about my new campaign, ERP. After his teachings, I became the subject matter expert on ERP. I was also a legend for *volunteering* to do a presentation on ERP; that had never happened at the company.

Cold calling would become a strength of mine not necessarily because I was naturally good at it, but I got help from other people to learn a new skill. The criminal knew that Jesus would help him in the same way if he only did one thing: repent. In my career, my cold calling improved even more. At my next company, Libelle, I produced so many leads that our rival company, SAP, had to send a notice saying that we could not say anything negative about their competing product. I worked for a small investment company down the hall while at Libelle, and, during that time, I produced many leads for that company, one of which nearly turned into a $6 million dollar M&A deal. Because of my success, I started to help coach the Morehouse Sales Team at age 26. At age 27, I interviewed to train 700 inside sales reps at Oracle, one of the most powerful business software giants in the world. I don't say all of this to brag; I tell you it to illustrate why you can't ever just give up. Proverbs 24:10 tells us that "If you falter in times of trouble, how small is your strength." Whatever you are going through, you must remember the sage words of Ronald Reagan when he said. "It can be done." Trouble may be something you hope to avoid in life, but if you never had trouble in your life, success would never have any meaning. Only in getting through that trouble is success truly success.

*

Failing should be thought of like a photograph. You see it, but only for the instant in which the image was captured. Photography can be misleading, just like failing. If you were to take a picture of Jordan Spieth at The Masters Tournament before the 12th hole meltdown in 2016, you would have seen a cool and collected young man getting ready to win back to back green jackets. Moments later, if you were to take an image of him chunking a shot into the water on that hole, you would have thought he was an amateur. It is tough as humans to remember that failures are just images; they are not the whole story, however. As painful as Jordan's experience was at The Masters that year, in *The Joy Luck Club* by Amy Tan, Lindo has one that is just as bad if not worse. She is a young Chinese girl who is betrothed into a marriage where her husband is a lazy, whiny, little boy who treats her like trash. Despite all of this, she still has an inner resolve that Spieth has after he had choked. Right before she gets married, she says these simple, but bold words: "I wiped my eyes and looked in the mirror. I was surprised at what I saw. I had on a beautiful red dress, but what I saw was even more valuable. I was strong. I was pure. I had genuine thoughts inside that no one could see, that no one could ever take away from me. I was like the wind.

I threw my head back and smiled proudly to myself… I would never forget myself."

Spieth never did forget himself. Despite being the focal point of one of the most epic collapses in major championship history, he still conducted himself like a gentleman, still made you think that in a world that often seems so sick and twisted, there are still men out there like Spieth who you want your son to be like one day. Failing is not failure; how you react to your failure is the indication of whether you have truly failed or not. I'll never forget how Spieth reacted in his ensuing press conference and trophy presentation. It's how we all should react once we fail. Not only did his humble nature show through, but also his belief for something greater than himself, just like the criminal on the cross. Even more impressive is that the year after he failed, when he hit a shot to the green on No. 12, he raised his hands jokingly, having the humility to poke fun at himself for what had happened.

Jack Nicklaus, the best golfer of all-time and winner of 6-green jackets, said this after Spieth's collapse: "My heart goes out to him for what happened, but I know Jordan is a young man who will certainly learn from this experience and there will be some good that comes out of this for him." While Spieth has and will learned from what happened, I would put the emphasis off of what he learned and instead on what he *taught* us all that day: character.

I have a feeling when Jordan finds out that he was included in this book that primarily deals with character, his response will be eerily similar to that of Bobby Jones—founder of the Masters— who deflected the laudatory comments he received for famously calling a shot on himself during the 1925 US Open. After the round, when reporters went on and on about his integrity, Jones simply quipped: "you might as well praise a man for not robbing a bank."

One other reason that Spieth knew he couldn't throw a temper tantrum is because it would have completely taken the attention off the winner, Danny Willet, and put all the attention on himself instead. Spieth didn't want this. This selflessness will serve young Jordan Spieth well in the coming years. Even if he doesn't win another green jacket—which I find highly unlikely at this point—he will have earned the respect of former Masters champions such as Arnold Palmer, Jack Nicklaus, as well as Payne Stewart, who never won a Masters, but who is considered one of the greatest gentleman to play the game of golf; the PGA sportsmanship award is named after him. Most of all, in his actions, Spieth demonstrated the major ideal I highlight in my first book, *Forget Self-Help*, which is selflessness.

In the same vein, I'm astonished when I hear Jordan Spieth use first person plural pronouns such as "we" and "us" when talking about golf rounds as opposed to the first-person singular pronoun "I" and "my." He does this to take the emphasis off himself once again and share the credit of his success with caddie Michael Greller. The world of sports that we live in today absolutely sickens me. It seems that when an individual does do something noteworthy, he tries to capture the limelight for himself. On the contrary, it's refreshing that an individual who is so talented as Spieth tries to deflect praise like a Gore-Tex[4] jacket deflects rain.

Unselfishness and character run in tandem; you cannot have one without the other. Just like no one has made that big of a deal out of Jordan's character that day, Spieth can rest assured that no

---

[4] **Gore-Tex** is a waterproof, breathable fabric membrane and registered trademark of W. L. Gore and Associates. Invented in 1969, Gore-Tex is able to repel liquid water while allowing water vapor to pass through and is designed to be a lightweight, waterproof fabric for all-weather use.

one has written or admired the Criminal on the Cross as much as I have. After all, he is so obscure in The Bible that he doesn't even have a name. To me, the more obscure an act is, the stronger position it has on the character scale, or, as I say in *Forget Self-Help*, "When judging another person, I never look for the big moments that test their character. I look for the small ones. Big moments carry a heroic aspect to them so there is a certain selfish incentive to make sure they are carried out to fruition. Small moments, however, never get any credit. This accentuates their value."

And to conclude, when Jordan was asked by the media after the round to sum up his feelings, he didn't chuckle and try to laugh it off, or on the other hand, get angry and throw a temper-tantrum. He simply said with complete transparency, "this one will hurt. It will take a while." I can't say for certain if Spieth listened to "I'm Real" by Jennifer Lopez featuring Ja Rule to this song when it first came out in 2001 considering he was eight; nonetheless, he seemed to understand J Lo's message crystal clearly when she preaches, to be genuine One thing is for certain: you'll always get respect for being authentic. Those who are afraid to be seen that way can't go anywhere, for no one will put trust in fool's gold, not even a fool. We will never see someone conduct himself on the golf course like Jordan Spieth did for a while or ever; he's one of the outliers.

But wait, there's one more thing he showed during that day: gratitude. Even at the tender age of 22, he would not take it for granted that he was on golf's most hallowed grounds. Even though he didn't win that day, through his actions, he was still appreciative of getting to compete on golf's biggest stage, one that many in the world would love to compete on. He showed just why the Masters is called a tradition unlike any other.

*

In *Flowers for Algernon*, the book is structured by the progress reports that Charlie, the retarded man, writes for the reader. In his first progris[5] (progress) report, he cuts right to the chase: he wants to become smart. He writes, "I hope they use me becaus Miss Kinnian says mabye they can make me smart. I want to be smart." In his second progris (progress) report, he reveals that he experienced a failure: "I had a test today. I think I faled it and I think mabye now they wont use me." It interesting, I hope I live up to God's expectations and just as Charlie is disappointed, I am disappointed when I let down God. Luckily for me, however, I know that I am not a failure in His eyes because of his Son. I often want to do things on my own, however, and achieve greatness on my own. That's not the way it works in Christianity, and I'm glad about that, because on my own I would fail—but with Christ, I know that I cannot possibly fail.

Charlie has a keen fascination with becoming smart. He truly believes that once he gains this intelligence, all his worries go away. He says things like, "If your smart you can have lots of friends to talk to and you never get lonely by yourself all the time." He wonders, "What do smart pepul think about or remember. Fancy things I bet. I wish I new some fancy things already."

Later on in the novel, "Frank laffed and said dont get so eddicated that you wont talk to your old friends. I said dont worry I will always keep my old friends even if I can read and rite. He was laffing and Joe Carp was laffing but Gimpy came in and told them to get back to making rolls. They are all good friends to me."

Charlie does eventually obtain intelligence from the operation—a lot of it actually. In fact, he obtains so much intelligence that he

---

[5] There are misspellings on purpose.

can no longer communicate with his friends at the bakery. Irony is so powerful because it is not only like a fish swimming upstream, it is like a fish swimming upstream at the exact same speed as one swimming downstream, maybe even *faster*. In the same way, the more we admit our sin, the faster we swim. Most people think that admitting their faults would be the weak thing to do, but in actuality, this shows their strength.

*

"Learning to Fly," by Tom Petty and the Heartbreakers, is a song you've probably heard before. When it came out in 1991 by Tom Petty and the Heartbreakers, it reached #28 on the US *Billboard* Hot 100 charts. Below, I examine some of the lyrics that I have paraphrased.

By myself – Never have I ever felt so by myself than during the 48-hour stretch I was deeply depressed in the bleak December of 2016. I felt as if the whole world had abandoned me and no longer cared about me. Robert E. Lee spoke some words to his son that I have never forgotten and often give to people in their time of deep despair: "Shake off those gloomy feelings. Drive them away. Fix your mind & pleasures on what is before you... Do not dream. It is too ideal, too imaginary. Dreaming by day, I mean. Live in the world you inhabit. Look upon things as they are. Take them as you find them. Make the best of them. Turn them to your advantage." Sad thoughts, Lee observed, "will sometimes come over us.... They are the shadows to our picture. They bring out prominently the light & bright spots. They must not cover up all. They must not hide the picture itself." Use the shadows, Lee advised, "as a medium through which to view life correctly."

After that intense depression, however, my greatest achievement ensued when I published *Forget Self-Help*. It wasn't my greatest achievement in that I gained fame, made money or anything like that, it was my greatest achievement in that I changed lives; in changing lives, my own life was changed.

I can't fly – For whatever reason, many of us feel like we don't have wings or the capacity to propel ourselves forward. That's when we need to learn on one another for support. A classmate of mine from Westminster was with me during the dark and ominous night when I was deeply depressed. Without her, I might not have been alive to finish *Forget Self-Help* and, in turn, change people's lives. We can't achieve our goals all alone; we need to lean on others from time to time for support. That's another reason why it is so vital to fail from time to time growing up. This forces you to seek out help and ask for advice or a helping hand.

Ground zero - Once you have been at the pinnacle of your game, it is tough to realize that you are human, and you will fail at some point or another. The real question is, are you going to have the power to lift yourself back up? My favorite golfer still to this day is Tiger Woods. I grew up reading his biography by Matt Christopher. In short, I adored him. His fall from golf's most impressive golfer, to a player who couldn't even hit chips was tough for me to see. I was pleasantly surprised to see him come into form as of late. Although I was not as good as a golfer as Tiger Woods, I got to be pretty good in my mid-teens. I broke 155 on 36 holes quite a bit and even shot a 30 on 9 holes in competition. Today, I am fortunate to make a few pars in a round of 18 holes. To be down all the time is tough, but to have had that glimmer of hope once you were up and come straight down is truly the hardest thing.

Things might not get better – Our past should never define our future. We always have a chance to have good days ahead of us as long as we have the ability to serve others. My favorite story on this topic was told to me by a psychiatrist during one depression I had when I was unemployed in the winter of 2017. He told me of a little girl who had just been diagnosed with an illness that would end her life soon. Despite her prognosis, she was still very energetic and as upbeat as one could possibly be in that condition. People asked her why she was this way… The reason for this she said is that "God is crying with me." We often hear one of the more famous passages quoted in times of trouble, Jeremiah 29:11: "For I know the plans I have for you," declares the Lord, "plans to prosper you and not to harm you, plans to give you hope and a future." Although this passage is comforting, I believe it is the most misused passage in all of the Bible. To me, it almost reads, "toughen up kid, things will get better!" This doesn't exactly help me during my time of need, but hearing the little girl be encouraged enough that we have a God who is empathetic to cry with us, does.

Take the first step – Many times, we have no idea where we are going. Martin Luther King Jr. once said, "Take the first step in faith. You don't have to see the whole staircase, just take the first step." Taking the first step can be hard sometimes, but all we need to do is to live in the way that Robert E. Lee advises us to do when he says, "get correct views of life, and learn to see the world in its true light. It will enable you to live pleasantly, to do good, and, when summoned away, to leave without regret." What are correct views? Well, just knowing that the world is not all about you and is about others is a good start. What does it mean to see the world in its true

37

light? Seeing it through the lens of a contributing instead of receiving is paramount to seeing the world in its true light. Doing good is such an important part of our life, and I feel as if some Christian traditions teach us to stay away from doing bad more than they teach us to do good. This is a shame because we fail to show people that we are the light of the world as Luke 8:16 tells us: "no one lights a lamp and hides it in a clay jar or puts it under a bed. Instead, they put it on a stand, so that those who come in can see the light."

Courage often is a result of failure in the same way that success is a result of courage. Therefore, to achieve success in life, you have to overcome failure with courage. The criminal was down to the wire—just about to die. In admitting he had let Jesus down, he admitted failure. In doing so, he was as courageous as ever.

2

Opening Up

Again, in *The Joy Luck Club*, by Amy Tan, an example is shown where a young girl in the story is just like the Criminal. She is away on vacation with other relatives when she gets lost, away from her friends and family. She sees the Moon Lady as she is called and longs to give her a wish.

"I have a wish! I have one!" I shouted as I ran forward in my bare feet. But the young man paid no attention to me and walked off the stage. I kept running toward the moon to tell the Moon Lady what I wanted, because now I knew what my wish was. I darted fast as a lizard behind the stage, to the other side of the moon.

I saw her, standing still for just a moment. She was beautiful, ablaze with the light from a dozen kerosene lamps. And then she shook her long shadowy tresses and began to walk down the steps.

"I have a wish," I said in a whisper, and she did not hear me. So I walked closer yet, until I could see the face of the Moon Lady:

shrunken cheeks, a broad oily nose, large glaring teeth, and red-stained eyes. A face so tired that she wearily pulled off her hair, her long gown fell from her shoulders. And as the secret fell from my lips, the Moon Lady looked at me and became a man.

But now that I am old, moving every year closer to the end of my life, I also feel closer to the beginning. And I remember everything that happened that day because it has happened many times in my life. The same innocence, trust, and restlessness, the wonder, fear, and loneliness. How I lost myself.

I remember all these things. And tonight, on the fifteenth day of the eighth moon, I also remember what I asked the Moon Lady so long ago. I wished to be found.

The only way to be found is to admit we are lost. It's hard to do this, however. In interview prep, we are taught to focus on our strengths, and, if we do have a weakness, we are told to spin it into a positive. In Matthew 11:28-30, however, Jesus says that, "Come to me, all you who are weary and burdened, and I will give you rest. Take my yoke upon you and learn from me, for I am gentle and humble in heart, and you will find rest for your souls. For my yoke is easy and my burden is light." Here, Christ tells us to "lose our self" just as Ying Ying loses herself in the story. Why are we so often afraid to lose our self? The number one reason is pride; in many ways, in the meritocratic society we live in, it is tough to admit our downfalls, tough to admit our faults. When we do, however, we are one with God and can start living in the way he imagined we should live.

One of my favorite Dave Matthews' songs is in the same vein of Matthew 11:28-30. It is called "Pantala Naga Pampa." The lyrics are as comforting as a mother's touch during a child's bout with the flu.

Calm yourself now
Lay down those tough thoughts
You can lean on others for support
Trust me, you can

"Calm yourself now" – Ultimately, once we repent, all we need to do is relax because there is no more work for us to do. I am often pensive with worldly things when I should be content with knowing that there is nothing to do. But, in some way, I am insulted by the cross. Especially in the United States, we live in a meritocracy where the best performance gets rewarded. In Christianity however, the opposite takes place because of the blood of Jesus. Even though this is the case, it is often times challenging for very rich, powerful, or intelligent people—when I mean wealthy, I mean newer money, not inherited old money—to accept Christ because they are truly impressive in their own right, and they had to work their tail off. In their field, they have accomplished all there is to accomplish—without assistance from anyone. This is the reason it is challenging for them to accept Christ; after all, they are not used to asking for help.

"Lay down those tough thoughts"- This is one of the hardest things for me to do. I am always seeming to worry, unfortunately more often than not on selfish desires instead of the desires of The Lord. In Matthew 6:25-34, Jesus says: "Therefore I tell you, do not worry about your life, what you will eat or drink; or about your body, what you will wear. Is not life more than food, and the body more than clothes? Look at the birds of the air; they do not sow or reap or store away in barns, and yet your heavenly Father feeds them. Are you not much more valuable than they? Can any one of

41

you by worrying add a single hour to your life? "And why do you worry about clothes? See how the flowers of the field grow. They do not labor or spin. Yet I tell you that not even Solomon in all his splendor was dressed like one of these. If that is how God clothes the grass of the field, which is here today and tomorrow is thrown into the fire, will he not much more clothe you—you of little faith? So do not worry, saying, 'What shall we eat?' or 'What shall we drink?' or 'What shall we wear?' For the pagans run after all these things, and your heavenly Father knows that you need them. But seek first his kingdom and his righteousness, and all these things will be given to you as well. Therefore do not worry about tomorrow, for tomorrow will worry about itself. Each day has enough trouble of its own."

What this verse is saying is not to worry about earthly things, but rather things worth chasing after, like the character traits that the Criminal had. In my life, when I have failed to have the character necessary, it has been chasing after things that do not bring glory to The Lord. These things might be success, fame, money, and other worldly things. Worry in itself is not a bad thing; we need to be careful of what we are ultimately worrying about, however. You want to have your worries to be in parallel with the Lord—not in parallel with the worries of man.

Robert E. Lee once said, "The march of Providence is so slow and our desires so impatient; the work of progress so immense and our means of aiding it so feeble; the life of humanity is so long, that of the individual so brief, that we often see only the ebb of the advancing wave and are thus discouraged. It is history that teaches us to hope." We all hope; it is what we hope for that demonstrates where our true heart is. All the criminal hoped for was to be found again; in his repentance and in his character, that happened.

"You can lean on others for support" – Being weighed down while you are trying to move swiftly is one of the worst feelings in the world. It is such a hopeless feeling because you know if the weight were to be removed, you would be free. In the same way, the Criminal looked to Jesus by being humble, honest, and strong enough to admit his faults. When we follow the criminal's action, we, too, are not only free, but are empowered to move in a swifter, more powerful way.

"Trust me, you can." – What happens when somebody says, "sit back, relax, and enjoy the show?" You are immediately at ease; you are in another zone. You're in a zone where you can forget about the 100 emails you have to answer, a zone where you have a trusted babysitter at home with the kids, and, most of all, a zone where your focus is not on your troubles. The criminal realized he could achieve this with Jesus and jumped on the opportunity. God is that trusted babysitter; he will let nothing go beyond where you can't handle it; he loves us that much. Falling away is one of the most vulnerable actions that a human can take. The reason for this is simple: it means putting your trust in something other than yourself. At first, it's hard, but minute by minute, and day by day, it becomes easier. With Christianity, the less you are in control, the more you are in control.

Oftentimes, it's easy to feel like you have no way out. In his 2004 song, "Locked Up," Akon describes a similar scenario that we face every day in our sin. He raps, "I'm trying to figure out things, why do I take the actions I take?, Getting out of these metal bars isn't coming sooner, it doesn't depend on what I do." Akon is right; with only ourselves to free ourselves, we will never be free. Only when we display the necessary character traits that the criminal possessed, can we find freedom. I often wonder why I do what I do just like Akon does in this song, but in the end, it doesn't matter because in Christ, I find perfect freedom.

As Tim Keller says in *Counterfeit Gods*, "You don't realize Jesus is all you need until Jesus is all you have." Sometimes my faith fluctuates depending on how things are going in my life. This is only natural because when I am having a lot of success, I don't feel as if I need God, for I feel as if I can accomplish anything; only when I struggle is when I ask God for the most help. This shouldn't be the case, however, because regardless of our circumstances, we always need God even if we become an instant success overnight. When we feel we are no longer needing of God's grace, there is one person tricking us: the Devil.

"Trust me, you can." – God calls us to be our troubles down each and every day. With him, we rest in perfect peace.

*

"I felt tired and foolish, as if I had been running to escape someone chasing me, only to look behind and discover there was no one there." – Jing-Mei-Woo, *Joy Luck Club*

The nice thing about knowing that Jesus died for our sins is that once we know that simple truth, our lives are transformed. Sin is no longer chasing us; we no longer have to dodge and weave to hide; we are free, but only if we admit our sin. In every sense of the word, Jing-Mei-Woo had failed. She failed to corral a husband, she failed to get her college degree, and, most of all, she had failed to win the approval of the one she longed to get the most: her mother.

*

Although I am young, I have found in my early career and in life that people—including myself—try to hide their weaknesses or blind spots in hopes that you do not see them even though people always do. Mark 4:22 says, however, "for everything hidden is meant to revealed, and everything concealed is meant to be brought to light."

In *Forget Self-Help*, I say "one reason that we never get to know other people is because it requires us to become vulnerable to other people and to become vulnerable not only requires work, but also requires courage. Rarely will you meet someone who is willing to admit his blind spots, willing to admit his flaws. However, when this happens, a whole new world is opened up because it enables both parties to be genuine with each other."

The most apparent example of somebody opening themselves to the world and becoming vulnerable happened in December of 2017 of my life. I opened up Facebook and noticed a picture of a girl in Paris in front of the Eiffel tower I had been on a couple dates with four years ago. Instead of describing what she says in the photo, I have left the unedited Facebok post below:

Solo in the city of love, yet I feel like dancing and making strangers laugh 💃🕺💚💚

*

Life came full circle as I stood in the city of love & romance. Where people come to "lock-in their love forever." After a year of unfathomable heartache, being unwanted and replaced by the person I loved most. Months filled with tears & pain, after fully loving with all that I had. The past couple of months have been the hardest of my life and the journey has been every bit of difficult...but I can finally say I am starting to feel real peace. No my heart isn't healed & the pain hasn't left; but I can finally feel God's arms wrapped around me tightly and he has given me a taste of the peace & comfort I have been begging him for. I knew the holidays were going to be hard and that's been proven to be true, as all of the engagements of loved ones unfold and sometimes being at the right place at the wrong time…as I stood in front of a Christmas tree in a town center of another country next to a couple as they got engaged, then here at the top of the Eiffel Tower, standing right next to another couple as the man got down on one knee. Seeing people experiencing the happiest moment of their lives thus far, feelings and a scenario I had experienced myself a year ago, but now watching as an outsider, was definitely salt in the wound. I heard recently, "the holidays illuminate being lonely, who you miss & what you miss" I've fallen into the comparison trap of trying to force myself to heal quicker, because time has passed, because the other has long moved on, but I've learned we all have to heal at our own pace. I am finally on the climb out of the valley but it's here, as we reach for our breakthrough, that the enemy tries to overcome us with our weakness. I am still weak but thank goodness my God is strong.

*

You never know how tough the holidays can be for some people; everyone has their own battle going on and sometimes during the holidays the battle is the fiercest. So share a smile, a hug or a dance with a stranger and spread joy to others, because it's truly contagious and just maybe, the more joy you spread the more joy you will feel.

Quite frankly, to have the gumption to post this on Facebook says a lot about Jane. It says a lot about her character, her intuition, and her ability to fight. I've honestly never witnessed anything like it my life. It's very similar to what our criminal who doesn't have a name did when he was on the cross next to Jesus. He admitted he was wrong, admitted had let God down, but most of all, he admitted that he was only human.

The only difference between Jane and the criminal is that she hadn't done anything wrong, and she still suffered this tragic fate.

The fact that she has such a positive attitude makes it all the more impressive. In making yourself vulnerable to the ones you love, a foundation as solid as a rock is formed. This happens because that person who opens up is essentially like a salesman who is telling you all the imperfections about themselves/product and hoping you still buy. This is the salesman you want to work with, but what salesman ever has your interest in mind enough to do this?

Compared to Jane, I had a similar experience happen to a college friend that went through a tough breakup; her attitude towards the break up was about as different as Jane's was. Because I tried to be a good friend, I asked her how she was doing, and she just said "that everything was fine and happened for a reason; God was in control." It was a typical token Christian answer; I had hoped that she would be more honest with me. She didn't open up to people, she wasn't vulnerable, and she didn't seek out help.

Admitting your blind spot is a challenging thing to do, but it produces a realness is relationships because it shows the person you know that you are only human. That humility opens the door for them to be humble back to you, opening the way for a deeper form of communication than you thought was possible. I always like to admit to people that I am not the smartest person in the room. I made a 330 on the GMAT, which is in the 14nd percentile[6]. When I tried to take the LSAT, I made a harrowing score coming in the 4th percentile on my practice test. I can also vividly remember going to back to an alumni function for high school in February of 2013 after I had recently graduated in December 2012. Somebody asked me what I was doing; my only reply was watching a ton of Seinfeld. I could have made up something, but I was comfortable enough in

---

[6] On the math section, I received in the 2nd percentile on Math.

my own skin to poke fun at myself. It makes life a lot more enjoyable for yourself and the people around you when you do this.

I often find myself trying to be perfect, and when I'm not, I find myself trying to cover up my sin when I should be doing the opposite because Christ died for me. I've often noticed other people trying to do this as well. It's almost as if they are building an awning to keep people from seeing their sin. Again, in *The Joy Luck Club*, there is a character named Waverly Jong. She takes up chess at an early age and is an absolute master at it. Her mother encourages her, but tries to take all the credit, much to the dismay of Waverly. After this happens one more specific time, she explodes and runs away. The book reads:

> I fled down an alley, past dark curtained shops and merchants washing the grime off their windows. I sped into the sunlight, into a large street crowded with tourists examining trinkets and souvenirs. I ducked into another dark alley, down another street, up another alley. I ran until it hurt and I realized I had nowhere to go, that I was not running from anything. The alleys contained no escape routes.

For us here on earth, life doesn't contain any escape routes until we repent. When we repent, we escape to a route that is tried and true, never to let us down. Admitting we are wrong, however, can be a challenging thing to do, especially when we are encouraged to pretend that everything we do is right. We can go from alley to alley, searching in vain to find certain the truth that will set us free. But if we look in the wrong places, we will be as foolish as Ponce de Leon who searched for the Fountain of Youth, but never found it. The last thing I like to do is admit that I am wrong, but when I do, I know God is smiling; after all, it means my complete trust is in him.

In order to be a strong Christian, it's not about going to Sunday School, going to winter retreats in the mountains, or going to Bible Study, it's about admitting you're wrong. You're wrong in the way you treat people, you're wrong in how you spend your money, and most of all, you've fallen short in being a man or woman after God's own heart. The criminal chose his own happiness because he was bold enough to admit he had screwed up. Why can't we be humble enough to do the same? As mentioned previously, in *Joy Luck Club*, by Amy Tan, there are a group of ladies that are Chinese immigrants who have left despair and ruin to come to San Francisco. Just like everyone, they have a choice to either be happy or sad, disappointed or eager. Luckily, they choose to be happy and eager and look forward to the lives they had ahead of themselves and chose their own happiness:

It's not that we had no heart or eyes for pain. We were all afraid. We all had our miseries. But to despair was to wish back for something already lost. Or to prolong what was already unbearable... What was worse, we asked among ourselves, to sit and wait for our own deaths with somber faces? Or to choose our own happiness.

Happiness lies in admitting our blind spots, our frailties; the weak man is the one who tries to hide them. *A River Runs Through It*, by Norman MacLean, runs a similar course as what was just described in *Joy Luck Club*. The book has special significance to me because it was the one book I asked for from my mother when I was in my only manic state in the summer of 2008. I was in Emory Hospital for 10 or 11 days. I knew deep down, I needed help just like the younger brother Paul needs help from his older brother, Neal. At first, I refused to take the medication, but eventually relented. At night, I would fall into a deep slumber as the anti-psychotic Seroquel took affect and numbed my whole body for hours. I got up to 800 mg at my highest point; now I take only 50 mg at night. It's still a deafening drug. Most mornings I wake up with a hangover even if I haven't had a sip of alcohol. It was help that I needed though and still need today. I am grateful for it, just like I am grateful for the cross.

In the book, both brothers live in Montana with their father. Their father is Presbyterian minister, and they go fly-fishing with him often. Neal writes … "As a Scot and a Presbyterian, my father believed that man by nature was a mess and had fallen from an original state of grace. Somehow, I early developed the notion that he had done this by falling from a tree. As for my father, I never knew whether he believed God was a mathematician but he certainly believed God could count and that only by picking up God's rhythms were we able to regain power and beauty. Unlike many Presbyterians, he often used the word "beautiful."" The real question is how do we become beautiful? The answer is very different depending on who you talk to. It might mean fitting into size 4 jeans if you're a young professional girl in a metropolitan city like New York, Boston, or Dallas. It might mean drawing a painting as unique and disruptive as an original Van Gogh painting. To God however, beauty means admitting we are broken and lost, needing to pick up God's rhythms to regain it. Whatever we do is not enough because we have all fallen short, so very short of his Glory. Only in the cross, can we regain that beauty.

3

Take Off Your Mask

The opposite of sarcasm is vulnerability. You can tell when a man is strong when he is more attuned to the latter rather than the former. At one point, in *A Separate Peace*, by John Knowles, after Gene makes a sarcastic response to Phineas, he says, "It was only long after that I recognized sarcasm as the protest of people who are weak." I have never met a person in real power or authority who is sarcastic. It is only the people who have been posing as such I have found to be the most sarcastic. Telling someone how you really feel takes courage—a courage that is not within most of us. When Jesus is about to die, it is the other criminal who mocks Jesus who is sarcastic when he says in Luke 23:46: "Aren't you the Christ? Save yourself and us!" The other criminal, whose name is on this book, responds with "Don't you fear God, since you are under the same sentence? We are punished justly, for we are getting what our deeds deserve. But this man has done nothing wrong." In *Daring Greatly*, by Brene Brown, she says, "Vulnerability sounds like truth and feels like courage. Truth and courage aren't always comfortable, but they're never weakness." She's right; when truth isn't exactly on your side, it can be challenging to succumb to the bleak reality to whatever you're facing. Being courageous is never comfortable but challenging. They are never weakness, though; they are only strength. Atticus Finch says in *To Kill a Mockingbird*, "simply because we were licked a hundred years before we started is no reason for us not to try to win." Just out of principle, sometimes you have to fight. I've noticed, that in a true family, one person's fight for the other member of a family's dream gets to a certain point where they are fighting more for that family member's dream than their own dream. That is what true love is about. Speaking of love, in *P.S. I love you*, H. Jackson Brown Jr. says, "Twenty years from now you will be more disappointed by the things that you didn't do than by the ones you did do. So throw off the bowlines. Sail away from the safe harbor. Catch the trade winds in your sails. Explore. Dream. Discover." Sometimes you've got to go for it even if the odds are stacked up against you. In losing yourself you'll often find that you will become found instead of being continually lost. We stop worrying once we admit that we're lost. It's counterintuitive, but true.

In one of the newest hottest shows in TV today, *13 Reasons Why*, a town is ravaged by the suicide of a young high school girl. What's even worse is that Alex, another student, tries to commit suicide. Luckily, he fails in the attempt. He is still damaged by the attempt, however, and has to walk with a cane. An unlikely friend who is a jock decides to help him out by giving him physical therapy in the pool. Despite his help, tensions often rise between the two until one moment. In what is the most poignant scene I have seen since the courtroom scenes in both *To Kill a Mockingbird* and *A Time to Kill*, Zach displays what it is like to give help, and Alex displays what it is like to receive help. There is an upcoming dance, and Alex is worried how he will dance with his new girlfriend, Jessica. Zach quickly gets Alex standing up and shows just how exactly the two will dance together by him playing the role of Jessica. Zach tells Alex that all he has to do is lean into her. This scene is brilliant because it shows that when we are humble enough to accept help, only good things ensue.

Good movies teach us a lesson, even if they're a chick flick. In *He's Just Not That Into You*, a star studded cast of Jennifer Anniston, Bradley Cooper, Ben Affleck, Scarlet Johnassen, Drew Barrymore, and others live in Baltimore. They spend much of their time analyzing one another's love life, or lack thereof. My favorite character by far in the movie is Gigi. She's cute, but super awkward, even more awkward than I am around girls, which is saying a great deal. Alex is a bar manager she meets one night when she is apparently supposed to have a date with another man, Connor. What she is really doing there is hoping that she will run into him there. Alex knows Connor and even offers to call him, but Gigi is afraid that he will blow her cover. Gigi's excuse for wanting to see Connor is to give him back a pen that he supposedly left from a dentist. Alex refutes that statement by telling her that Connor's dentist is his father. Gigi is embarrassed once again, but a friendship is formed that night.

Alex invites Gigi over to a party he is hosting a few weeks later. Gigi misreads Alex's intentions as romantic instead of just friendship and embarrasses herself by trying to kiss Alex on the couch, which he does not appreciate one bit. She's embarrassed herself, but she did not lose that night, Alex did. I had never seen the whole movie until I recently had to watch it to write this book, but it has stuck with me all of these years:

I·may dissect each little thing and put myself out there so much but at least that means that I still care. Oh! You've think you won because women are expendable to you. You may not get hurt or make an jerk of yourself that way but you don't fall in love that way either. You have not won. You're alone. I may do a lot of stupid crap but I'm still a lot closer to love than you are.

When you're vulnerable, like Gigi was in this movie and how the criminal was that one night, you open yourself up to a lot of pain. I've learned through the years that risk is worth it, however. If you don't risk through going through that pain, you will never have meaningful relationships with others, whether that be just friendship or romantic. And if that's the case, how can you expect to have a meaningful relationship with God if you're not vulnerable? It's indefensible, unnecessary, and most of all, impossible.

Earlier in the movie, Gigi has a revelation. She learns that there are rules and that there are exceptions to the rules. In 99% of cases, the rule is what ends up happening. Alex eventually starts having feelings for Gigi, and in fact, turns into her. He constantly looks at his phone to see if she has called, and he starts to become awkward just like her. One night he decides to pay her a visit.

Gigi: [*opens the door, thinking it's Bill*] Did you forget something?
Alex: Yeah...
Gigi: Really? What did you forget?
Alex: [*pulls out a promotional pen from his pocket*] This.
Gigi: So you came all the way here at 11 o' clock in the night to give me a promotional pen?
Alex: Yeah... Yeah, I did. I thought I would come up with some really great excuse to get over here. That's how it's done, right?
Gigi: [*smiles*] Sometimes.
Alex: Look, I can't stop thinking about you. I... It's a problem. I drive by your place; I call and hang up; I've turned into...

Gigi: Me.

Alex: Yeah.

Gigi: A wise person once told me that if a guy wants to be with a girl, he will make it happen, no matter what.

Alex: That's true.

Gigi: But when I was hurling my body onto yours, you did not seem to want to make it happen.

Alex: Okay, yeah, here's the thing about that... You were right. I'd gotten so used to keeping myself at a safe distance from all these women and having the power that, that I didn't know what it felt like when I actually fell for one of them... I didn't know.

Gigi: Look, I just went out with your friend Bill. He might be just exactly what I need. No drama, he calls; he does what he says...

Alex: [*stepping closer*] I can do that stuff too...

Gigi: But you didn't! And that same wise person told me that I'm the rule. That I have to stop thinking that every guy will change, that I have to stop thinking that...

Gigi: [*Alex kisses her*]
[*smiles*]

Gigi: ... I'm the exception...

Alex: [*whispers*] You are *my* exception.
[*they kiss again*]

Just as Gigi is Alex's exception to the rule, in the same way, once you accept Christ into your life, you become the exception to the rule as well. Luke 6:23 says, "for the wages of sin is death; but the gift of God is eternal life through Jesus Christ our Lord." One of my favorite hymns is "Amazing Grace." I love it because in the hymn, there is a line that says, "amazing grace, how sweet the sound, that saved a wretch like me." Can you become vulnerable enough to God and to others to call yourself something as disgraceful as a wretch? I've noticed when I have, a whole new world opens up. In admitting I am lost, I become free.

Another one of my favorite moments of vulnerability occurs in one of my favorite movies of all time, *The Big Short*. One of the main characters, Michael Burry, is an egotistical, brilliant, economist, who has a reputation for picking stocks that go from low to high. He has a crazy, wild hunch in 2007 to do something that people thought was downright insane: bet against the housing market. When he does so, he is completely disrespected. He risks it all, yet even in the darkest hour, he still believes in himself. When he ends up being right, no one dares to talk to him, except through lawyers. That's when he says one of the quotes that will go down in history as the most vulnerable and honest quotes of all time:

I met my wife through Match.com. My profile said, "I am a medical student with only one eye, an awkward social manner, and $145,000 in student loans." She wrote back, "You're just what I've been looking for." She meant "honest", so let me be honest. Making money is not like what I thought it would be. This business kills the part of life that is essential, the part that has nothing to do with business. For the past two years, my insides have felt like they've been eating themselves. All the people that I respected won't talk to me anymore, except through lawyers. People want an authority to tell them how to value things, but they choose this authority not based on facts or results. They choose it because it feels authoritative and familiar. And I am not, nor ever have been, "familiar." So...so I have come to the sullen realization that I must close down the fund. Sincerely, Michael J. Burry, M.D.

The criminal was the same way. He had failed people; he had failed God. But he still had a choice to make. Would he pretend like it never happened, or would he own up to his mistakes like a man? He chose the former, and because he did, he was the first one allowed to heaven. Why in the world do we look at vulnerability as a weakness? I can remember one date I had a girl opened up to me that she might not be able to have kids because of a medical condition. It was incredible that she would open up to me that early on, for we had not even formed a true relationship. I've learned, within certain limits, to never be afraid to open up to other people about your faults or anything different about you that you were born with. Those people who can't accept you for who they are not people who you want to be around, anyway. To be frank, they have no heart and are the opposite of what the criminal was like.

I have not been successful in the dating arena for many reasons. When I was younger, I used to brag about my accomplishments too much. Additionally, as good as I am with people, for whatever reason, I've always been socially awkward around girls ever since I was young. One of the chief reasons, however, is that I struggle mightily with playing games and feel disrespected when girls play games with me. What's the point? Why can't we just be genuine with each other from the onset? That's why when I was texting with a girl who I had met on a dating app, I was stunned by how vulnerable she was towards me; I was also attracted to it.

Here are the texts below:

Girl: Want total honesty?

Me: Sure, why not? It seems like we are both being honest with each other

Girl: Ha so strange

Me: So go ahead and tell …

Girl: Nah I'll save my weirdness for like my psychiatrist ha

Girl: I broke up with someone recently and downloaded apps in a weird moment of insecurity and doubt … why I said I'm not in a neat place

Granted, she had looked up my book and seen that I wrote a book that does touch on depression, but, still, the openness and honestly was incredible. I am so used to girls waiting seven hours to text back to show that they're not too interested, so it was quite refreshing to get some honesty from someone. I've also had a girl who I knew quite well in a romantic fashion not only not answer when I called her, but not call me back or text me back when we *specifically* set up a time to talk one Friday night. I would text her a few days later wondering what happened, and she texted me back a whole day later with "I'm sorry, I feel awful." When I asked her what had happened, she said she was too busy to even send me back a text that would have taken her 15 seconds to compose.

Who do you think would have a higher propensity to have a divorce later on? The first girl with all her problems or the second girl who cannot be properly trusted? The criminal had problems, but he could be trusted. In the same way, God wants us to admit our problems to him. When we do, he trusts us more because we change from being inauthentic to authentic. It's ironic how it works out, but true.

4

The Truth ~~Hurts~~ Helps

Without integrity, a person is empty. The emptiness comes from that person's lack of respect for reality; in life, reality accounts for everything that is worthwhile. One of my proudest moments came in 10th grade at the college preparatory school I attended, The Westminster Schools. Like many strong schools in the South, Westminster had a very strong honor system. I was an Alpha Omega at Westminster, meaning that I started going to school there in Pre-1st. This meant that by 10th grade, my parents, (or grandparents), had spent approximately $130,000 on me to go there. While I did well in elementary school and for part of Junior High, my grades started to plummet by the time I hit high school. In the spring of that year, I was taking chemistry with a teacher called Mrs. Sconzo. She rarely taught "regular" students but did so this year. She wrote AP Tests on the side. Her class to this day is one of the hardest things I have ever been through. We were assigned a take home test to complete by yourself, but everybody was cheating off one student while the teacher was out of the room—everyone except me. I was already failing or close to failing at the time, but I could not bring myself to cheat like everyone else. I couldn't had lived with myself if I had. Later on, in the midst of the struggle in that class, I had to have a talk with my parents about possibly leaving the school and transferring schools. I told Mrs. Sconzo that people were cheating, but she said she couldn't do anything about it. Mrs. Sconzo and I kept in touch after all those years, and, one day, we reminisced with her about the test that everyone cheated on. She added a new bit of information, however. She told me that she intentionally counted that less because she knew everyone cheated: I guess I didn't get the memo.

In "Promoting a Culture of Academic Integrity" by Dr. Peggy Piascik and Dr. Gayle A. Brazeau, they talk about multiple issues surrounding a lack of integrity in the classroom. They bring up an interesting point when they say that, "the millennial generation is viewed as valuing efficiency and instant rewards. They are reported to be more concerned about outcome than process." I could see this easily being the case; in fact, I saw it time and time again throughout high school and college. I personally never cheated one time. I benefitted greatly from this most of all because I was able to see my strengths and weaknesses. I was forced to have a strong work ethic because school came as such a challenge. I was also forced to have an upbeat, positive personality because that was the only way I could survive at Westminster. Lastly, it taught me valuable selling skills to convince my teachers to pass me. Doing things the right way has its benefit in the long run. My career has been a testament to that.

Piascik and Brazeau later bring up an interesting point that, "As long as students view pharmacy and graduate school as just more hoops to jump through on the way to their degree, a culture of academic integrity will be difficult to establish in our educational programs ... Completing a pharmacokinetics problem set, answering enough multiple-choice questions correctly to get the desired grade, completing research papers, and preparing manuscripts or other assignments is not the ultimate objective. The goal must be in knowing how to take care of patients, keeping up-to-date with the latest advancements in therapy and the sciences, communicating effectively with other health professionals and scientists, devising the best possible solution to a therapeutic or research problem, and doing it all with compassion, enthusiasm, and dedication to the task." So many millennials today are obsessed with the final result, obsessed with the final grade that they are not willing to put in the effort that it takes to get that final result. As the article states, they are also used to instant gratification, which differs heavily from how generations before us dealt with such matters. In the 1950's, one man might start out a job and stay there until retirement; now millennials hop jobs every one or two years, sometimes even twice in one year. I've often heard a man's word used to mean something; that is not the case anymore.

In my work life, I have constantly tried to be forthright and upfront with potential clients for a few reasons. The first reason is that is the way I would want to be treated, and the second reason is more selfishly motivated: I know they are going to find out eventually if I am lying to them. One of my proudest moments of my short career was when I was working for a small company called Libelle. At age 25, I went down to Houston, TX to try and help close a software deal with oil juggernaut, Halliburton. The next part is a bit complicated, but I will try to explain it anyway. We had a previous prospect who was in a similar situation in that they outsourced the work that our software would do to a third-party, so it wouldn't make sense to use our product. My primary point of contact, Anthony, told me that they were doing the same thing, and, when he did, instead of keeping my mouth shut, I warned him that it make not make sense from a business standpoint for Halliburton to purchase our software. Out of 100 salespeople, not one would have been honest enough to tell him that, but I did. He then told me that's exactly why we needed to test out the software. We didn't end up closing the deal possibly due to the fact that oil was in a huge downturn, but I could tell that Anthony trusted me; that meant a lot.

Abraham Lincoln has long been known for his integrity. When he moved to Springfield Ilinois, he frankly told the new lawyers to "resolve to be honest at all events; and if in your judgment you cannot be an honest lawyer, resolve to be honest without being a lawyer. Choose some other occupation, rather than one in the choosing of which you do, in advance, consent to be a knave." Ironically, this is similar advice that Robert E. Lee gave to his son in a letter when he said, "Above all, do not appear to others what you are not." When we do try to appear to others what we are not, it is usually to circumvent a problem that we or others have. Rather than pretending it doesn't exist, attacking it head-on seems like not only the more sensible way to attack the problem but also the more expedient way. Pretending that something isn't wrong when something clearly is futile at best.

In a movie called *The Emperor's Club*, Mr. Hundert plays the role of Assistant Headmaster and Western History teacher at St. Benedict's Academy. He is a well-respected professor there; students adore him. One student he does have a problem with is Sedgewick Bell, a class clown whose father is a Senator with much influence over the school. Sedgewick is a horrible student until Mr. Hundert pushes him to compete for the Mr. Julius Caesar competition that is held at St. Benedict's every year. The competition is comprised of many students taking quizzes, with the top three students being placed on stage to compete for the crown. Despite the fact that Sedgewick knew the material, he cheats anyway. Years later, to avenge his loss, Sedgewick hosts all his former classmates up to his company's resort to have a re-match of the Julius Caesar competition. His character doesn't change; he cheats again and loses again. In the bathroom, Mr. Hundert confronts him again, just like he had done years before. He tells him:

"I'm a teacher, Sedgewick. And I failed you—as a teacher. But I will give you one last lecture, if I may. All of us, at some point, are forced to look at ourselves in the mirror, and see who we really are. And when that day comes for you, Sedgewick, you will be confronted with a life lived without virtue, without principle. And for that I pity you. End of lesson."

Sedgewick simply responds with, "Well, can I say, Mr. Hundert, who gives a care? Honestly. Who out there gives a crap? About your principles and your virtues? I mean, look at you. What do you have to show for yourself? I live in the real world where people do what they need to do to get what they want. And if it's lying and it's cheating, so be it. So I'm gonna go out there and I'm going to win that election, Mr. Hundert. And you'll see me everywhere. And I'll worry about my contributions later." Just as Sedgewick finishes his short speech, his young son walks out of the bathroom. He had heard everything. And, because he had heard everything, Sedgewick loses out on what he wants more than anything: the respect of his son.

Sedgewick needs to follow the sage words of Michael Jackson when he belted out "Man in the Mirror." The lyrics go, "I'm going to alter the things I do, for the first time in my life, I'm going to feel truly content, I'm going to make an impact, I'm going to set things on the correct path." To make a difference, we have to make a change. The reason for this is rather simple: we are all fallen—in need of his saving grace. Later, Michael Jackson sings, "Beginning with the guy in the mirror. I'm imploring him to alter his current actions, and I couldn't have been any more forthright. I've learned if you want to improve the world, improve yourself first." That act of telling yourself that you need to change your ways is the most manly and humble act there is. It is an honest act, too. Your interview for a job should be the exact opposite of how you approach your walk with God and others. I've been looking for jobs recently, and my best friend told me I need to be less honest with recruiters and hiring managers than I have been. Admittedly, in this dog-eat-dog world, that's how you have to be. Luckily, we don't have to be that way when it comes down to our relationship with God. God loves us for who we are when we admit that we are sinful.

Although I haven't made a ton of money the past few years, three out of the last four companies I have worked for have been former clients or prospects of mine at a company I worked for previously. I take great pride in that because it shows that I value relationships and integrity, something that is rare in most salespeople. There was one time, however, when I was much younger when I was selling bottled water outside Chastain Park Amphitheatre when I didn't do this. I was selling the water for $1.00 apiece when a lady asked me how much the water was. I thought I had the sale, so I told her $2.00. While it may not seem like a big deal to you what I did, to me it was utterly sinful; I even brought it up in an economics class at Samford years later. Like I said earlier, without integrity, a person is empty. The emptiness comes from that person's lack of respect for reality; in life, reality accounts for everything that is worthwhile. I had a lack of respect for reality, and because I did, my efforts that night were not worthwhile, but worthless.

Deepack Mahta, at the end of the movie says, "A great teacher has little external history to record. His life goes over into other lives. These men are pillars in the intimate structure of our schools. They are more essential than its stones or beams, and they will continue to be a kindling force and a revealing power in our lives." Recently, I was playing golf in Atlanta with my best friend from high school, and he was asking about my second book. I told him it was about the character traits of the criminal on the cross. He asked me what his name was, thinking that he should, in fact, know it. I told him that he did not have one. That's what makes him so special to me. Like Deepack said, the Criminal has little external history to record, but life goes into other lives. And he will surely be a kindling force and revealing power in our lives. He was the first because he admitted he was last.

Another example of my integrity occurred while I was a sophomore at Samford University. I had befriended an accounting teacher named Sharon Jackson and enjoyed her Financial Accounting class. As in all my classes, I was an active participant in class, often making comments that had to do with class, but also making other comments that were often in jest. With many students, people might get away with missing class, but if I were to miss class, I knew that she would notice. One night before class, I went with a few older fraternity brothers and had a little bit too much to drink. I felt bad for missing class and wanted to go into Mrs. Jackson to tell her why I missed class. Sure enough, when I went into her classroom, she was there wondering why I had missed class. I was honest with her and told her I was out drinking with friends of mine.

65

The point behind telling you all of this is not that the underage drinking is okay because it's not. My point behind telling you all of this is that Christ accepts us in our sin, just as Mrs. Jackson accepted me. It is only when we hide our sin that we get into trouble. Admitting your trouble is the surest way to get out of trouble in Christianity.

Because I drank the Vodka

In *Flight*, there is a scene which shows Captain Whip Whittaker is no longer going to lead a life of lies. Whittaker is a drunk who miraculously lands a failing plane but was drunk when it happened. Here is the dialogue from the NTSB hearing below:

Block: Is it your opinion that Katerina Marquez drank on that flight?

Whip: Could you repeat the question?

Block: Is it your opinion that Katerina Marquez drank on that flight?

Whip: I'm sorry, my what?

Block: Your opinion, Captain. Since her toxicology report is the only toxicology report is the only report that is admisable in this hearing, and she in fact tested positive for alcohol, is it your opinion that Katerina Marquez drank the two bottles of vodka on the plane?

Whip: *[exhales]* God help me.

Block: I'm sorry, Mr. Whittaker, I couldn't hear you. What did you say?

Whip: I said, "God help me."

Block: Yes, well, however, is it your opinion...

Whip: It's my opinion Trina did not drink that vodka.

Block: Excuse me, Mr. Whittaker?

Whip: She saved a boy's life.

Block: Could you speak louder, Mr. Whittaker?

Whip: Trina did not drink the vodka... because I drank the vodka.

In admitting he did the wrong thing, Whip does the right thing. It took courage, and he ended up going to jail, but he got what he could have never gotten had he kept it a secret: he got his life back. Additionally, he got the respect of his son back. He could also look himself in the mirror. You see, when we leave a life of lies, it not only hurts us, it hurts our family as well. In a letter to his son, Robert E. Lee once said, "you must study to be frank with the world, frankness is the child of honest courage." Being honest doesn't require you to be good-looking, smart, or clever, it only requires showing your authentic self to the world. Chances are if you are honest, people will appreciate you more, listen to you more, and value you more. The reason for this is simple: you will now be set apart in a rare class.

The biggest red flag to me in relationships is when people are inauthentic. Bill McDermott, former CEO of SAP, once said, "Authenticity is the currency of our time. It earns us respect and trust. Authenticity is also in demand, because it's rare." When I enter into a relationship with someone, I want to be able to completely trust them. Without trust in relationships, it is impossible to open up and become vulnerable because you're ultimately afraid they might use that against you. Being inauthentic doesn't just hurt yourself, it hurts others. It is also one of the biggest insults to God because it is telling Him that He does not have a plan for you to prosper; instead, that you, in fact, have to make your own plan.

George Washington once said, "I hope I shall possess firmness and virtue enough to maintain what I consider the most enviable of all titles, the character of an honest man." What do you envy? Is it success, or power? Here, the founder of our country challenges us to think about what matters most: integrity. Often times, I feel like society doesn't value this. Sedgewick, in *The Emperor's Club*, certainly doesn't. The Bible tells us in Proverbs 24:26 that, "an honest answer is like a kiss on the lips." I'm not surprised at all that The Bible tells us this. A kiss on the lips has an endearing quality to it, that no human interaction can match. If even only for that split second, people trust one another when they kiss; after all, you close your eyes. It's the type of trust that the criminal had in Jesus.

When It Is Okay to Lie

While this whole chapter is about encouraging you *not* to lie, there are some instances where it is noble to lie, but only when it is protecting someone else in an unselfish manner. One of my favorite songs growing up was "Drops of Jupiter (Tell Me)" by Train. When I was looking up the lyrics, the specific lyric that I wanted to use populated in Google it is so well known. The lyrics go like encourage you to stick up for your best friend even when you know they are incorrect.

The lyric reminds me of arguably the most poignant scene in *A Separate Peace* by John Knowles. Again, I like to use classics to illustrate important parts of the Bible because they can provide a clearer and more powerful illustration than The Bible itself can provide. It's not the that writers of the Bible weren't intelligent or deep, it's that classics provide them to us in everyday terms. In *Uncle Tom's*

Cabin, it paints a more than clear picture that the American type of slavery was wrong. In *To Kill a Mockingbird*, we can see that racism was rampant and widespread in their day. Even in *The Great Gatsby*, we can see Christ in Gatsby.

"I was thinking about you … and the accident."

"There's loyalty for you. To think about me when you were on a vacation."

"I was thinking about it … about you because – I was think you and accident because I caused it."

Finny looked steadily at me, his face very handsome and expressionless. "What do you mean, you caused it?" his voice was as steady as his eyes.

My own voice sounded quiet and foreign. "I jounced the limb. I caused it." One more sentence. "I deliberately jounced the limb so you would fall off."

He looks older than I had ever seen him. "Of course you didn't."

"Yes I did. I did!"

"Of course you didn't do it. You damn fool. Sit down, you damn fool."

"Of course I did."

"I'm going to hit you if you don't sit down."

"*Hit* me!" I looked at him. "*Hit* me! You can't even get up! You can't even come near me!"

"I'll kill you if you don't shut up."

"You see! Kill me! Know you know what it is! I did it because it felt like that! Now you know yourself!"

"I don't know anything. Go away. I'm tired and you make me sick. Go away." He held his forehead wearily, an unlikely way.

To Finny, athletics was his life. Because of what Gene did to him, that was no longer the case. How did he respond to his severe misfortune? Did he blame Gene for practically running his life? No, he didn't because he was stronger than Gene and knew that he still held a strong advantage over Gene even after being pushed off a limb and was nearly paralyzed. Lying is rarely seen as moral, but when that rare moment happens when you are sacrificing yourself for another, it is okay to do, even noble.

5

Less is More

For people who know me well, the irony that I am writing about humility is deafening. I might be one of the most arrogant human beings to walk the earth. The confidence has definitely helped me in sales, but it has also definitely hurt me in my personal relationships and romantic relationships (or lack thereof). The ultimate cause for the arrogance is pretty simple: I have a massive chip on my shoulder for multiple reasons and grew up failing a lot. I went to the preeminent high school in the South and had a massive learning disability that I was not prescribed medication for until I got to college. At one-point, sophomore year, I literally made a zero on a test even though I filled everything out. Things didn't get any better junior year when during one semester, I passed three of thirteen tests and quizzes in Math. I thought I was dumb and, because of this, struggled to find my identity in a culture where a high value was placed on intelligence.

Another reason I am insecure is because of the intelligence of my family. They have prestigious degrees from schools such as Harvard, Stanford, Columbia, Duke, Michigan, Vanderbilt, and others just to name a few. Around the dinner table, I could hardly get a word in and was constantly told I couldn't do this or that. I was deeply insecure about not getting into my state school as well, The University of Georgia. Even to this day, I am haunted by not getting in there despite the fact that I have had early success in my career.

One of the primary reasons for my insecurity occurred when I was diagnosed with bi-polar disorder. Although I absolutely love my alma mater, Westminster, there were a few people, both girls, that said very hurtful discriminating comments to me that absolutely killed me; I mean, killed me. I admit I might have a warped view of myself, but my arrogance came out of my insecurity for people from Westminster not thinking I could hold down a full-time job because of my disorder. I'm sure it is warped, but when I heard those two girls say those comments, I thought the whole world thought that. Arrogance and defensiveness often run in tandem with each other, so it's not surprising to admit that I often possess both.

When I did find worldly success, I found that my security grew deeper and deeper entrenched in it rather than The Lord. I became focused on things like country clubs, status, much of the time to prove to people I could in fact live a normal life. I should have been finding my security in Christ. Instead, I found my security in worldly things. Over and over however, those things let me down. Although I am a man and not a woman it reminded me of Proverbs 31:30: "Charm is deceptive, and beauty is fleeting; but a woman who fears The Lord is to be praised." The Buckhead life was deceptive; it engulfed me.

Even recently, I must admit that I became way too prideful of my writing when I published *Forget Self Help*. I originally published the book to help Christians grow closer to Christ and non-Christians to be introduced to Christ in an inoffensive, humble way. Soon, my focus became less on helping people and more focused on what other people thought of me because I was having success with the book. It's interesting the way the Devil can quickly turn a positive Godly thing into a negative evil one.

It's also interesting to note that the Criminal on the Cross possessed neither defensiveness nor arrogance; he was completely open and humble. Those two adjectives seem to work in one another. If you're humble, you're going to be open to other opinions and ways to live. If you're defensive, you're not only never going to open to either of these things, but you will also dig yourself into a deep hole that is impossible to get out of. The Criminal was open to a new way to live in Jesus; the one that mocks Jesus does not.

Furthermore, Matthew 18:1-5 says,

At that time the disciples came to Jesus and asked, "Who is the greatest in the kingdom of heaven?" He called a little child and had him stand among them. And he said, "I tell you the truth, unless you change and become like little children, you will never enter the kingdom of heaven. Therefore, whoever humbles himself like this child is the greatest in the kingdom of heaven. And whoever welcomes a little child like this in my name welcomes me." When we think of children, the last thing we think about is leadership. But if we think deeper, we realize that children are much more willing to learn than adults are. They haven't been in the world long enough to develop the egotistical mind-set that us adults have. Again, the irony in Jesus' statements is strong. Who in the world would think that when you humble yourself, you become more permanently stronger than ever?

In the same vein, Abraham Lincoln acted in a similar manner. In *Lincoln's Melancholy*, by Joshua Wood Shenk, Shenk writes, "Perhaps because our society is so influenced by advertising, which blurs the distinction between perception and reality, there is a sense today that people in positions of strength must never waver, never doubt themselves."

In my life, the times when I have been most open have been the times that have turned out to be the most successful. Only when we are open to other's perspectives on how we can live a better life will we find continuous and permanent improvement. You don't always have to do what is being told to you, but to not even listen hurts you more than it does anybody else. Accepting Jesus is not just a relationship; you are also forming a team. Kenneth Blanchard once said, "none of us is as smart as all of us." This is so true and to have the humility to choose Jesus shows how smart you are. Admitting I am broken and need Him was the most intelligent and impactful decision I have made my whole life. We're often told to "deny, deny, deny." We should instead be "admit, admit, admit," for this is what the criminal did.

While Abraham Lincoln was known for more of his confidence, he did something that David Bobb, author of *Humility: An Unlikely Biography of America's Greatest Virtue*, describes with C-SPAN moderator, Brian Lamb: Lincoln was willing to admit when he was wrong, and that's a rare thing. He wrote General Grant, even before the two men had ever met, a letter. They disagreed about what the General should do regarding Vicksburg. The general went ahead with his plan, and the President wrote him and said you know what, "I was wrong, you were right." Lincoln did that over and over again in his public life. Interestingly enough, the original title of this book was exactly that: *You're Right, I'm Wrong*. There is a disarming aspect of doing just that in relationships. Relationships become more real, more whole. We are all in the constant search for knowledge and in order to strengthen this search, we must often tell other parties that we are not always right.

One has to be humble to want to learn. The fact that you're reading this book in the first place means that you have some humility about you. You can tell when you're in true learning mode when you have the mentality that you can learn from anyone. When I went to my first Christian publishing conference, I was struck with how active the main speaker and famous writer, Brian McClaren, was fervently reading a new book that another, much less well-known author had written. I have found it interesting in my life that the more powerful a person is, often times, they are humbler than the people trying to climb their way to the top. In the same vein, when I was writing this book, I readily asked a young man to look over Chapter 1. He actually found some mistakes that enabled me to make it smoother and more readable.

To take learning even further, one has to learn from anybody and everybody, even the flawed. In doing so, your life will be changed, and once your life is changed, you will change others. This is why I include quotations from Robert E. Lee in my first and second book. He made the biggest mistake of his life by not upholding his pledge at West Point when he decided to fight for the South. To say that you cannot still learn something from Lee, however, doesn't make logical sense, for we are all flawed.

One of my favorite passages in the Bible is Matthew 8:5-13: The Faith of the Centurion. Like the Criminal on the Cross, the passage is fairly unknown, but if you implement its precepts to your faith walk, it could make a measurable difference.

When Jesus had entered Capernaum, a centurion came to him, asking for help. "Lord," he said, "my servant lies at home paralyzed, suffering terribly." Jesus said to him, "Shall I come and heal him?" The centurion replied, "Lord, I do not deserve to have you come under my roof. But just say the word, and my servant will be healed. For I myself am a man under authority, with soldiers under me. I tell this one, 'Go,' and he goes; and that one, 'Come,' and he comes. I say to my servant, 'Do this,' and he does it." When Jesus heard this, he was amazed and said to those following him, "Truly I tell you, I have not found anyone in Israel with such great faith. I say to you that many will come from the east and the west, and will take their places at the feast with Abraham, Isaac and Jacob in the kingdom of heaven. But the subjects of the kingdom will be thrown outside, into the darkness, where there will be weeping and gnashing of teeth."

Then Jesus said to the centurion, "Go! Let it be done just as you believed it would." And his servant was healed at that moment.

I love the fact that that he says, "Lord I do not deserve to have you come under my roof." The humility is astounding. Just like the Centurion, none of us deserve to have Jesus in our life. We have failed him in every way possible in the past, and we know that we will fail him again. But Jesus still loves us in our broken state; the proof is the action on the cross. Only when we admit that we are less, and He is more, will we be found. The reason for this simple: admitting that we are less doesn't make us less, it makes us more. What makes the Centurion that much more of an impressive figure is that he had all the power in the world with his position. With power, often comes pride. That pride is not from above, but down below. The only thing we need to be prideful of is what Jesus did for us on the cross. It was the opposite of prideful. Because of this, it was definition of powerful.

The next thing that Jesus tells the Centurion is how we should try to live every day of our life. He tells the Centurion "Truly I tell you, I have not found anyone in Israel with such great faith." He told the Centurion because he knew the Centurion knew the power that he had. Only when we understand that Jesus is in complete control can we start living life not to the fullest, but full of purpose. Our purpose starts being less about us and more about Him. The Centurion was exactly like the Centurion in that he understood Jesus' power and strength. That power and strength came from believing that he didn't have it all figured out, that he was only human.

Although I claim to not be a member of either mainstream party, I absolutely love presidential elections because I've been in sales the last five years. All political elections are sales, with the candidate who has strategized the best and put the most effort in. This isn't necessarily a bad thing, however, because to be a good politician, you have to be adept at selling. One thing I have yet to see from either political party in the last several years is the humble nature of perhaps our greatest president and founder, George Washington. Granted, George Washington didn't have to debate against several other potential candidates; he was appointed the job. Still, it seems like rather than attacking every other person on the debate stage, it could be prudent to even encourage one another on. My favorite part of the 2016 election was when Hillary Clinton and Donald Trump were forced to compliment one another. It showed their humbleness; it showed their grace. It's what George Washington would have done; it's what the criminal would have done.

When George Washington was elected President, he held the opposite belief that 100% politicians think when they get the job:

he, quite frankly, didn't think he was a good fit. Just imagine, despite the fact that he had just led the Colonies to miracle victory over Great Britain in the war for independence, he still thought himself inadequate for the job. When Washington went into Philadelphia on the way to the inauguration, he intentionally left Trenton an hour early, to avoid even the appearance of pomp or vain parade." He later said, "I greatly apprehend that my countrymen will expect too much from me," he wrote to Rutledge. "I fear, if the issue of public measures should not correspond with their sanguine expectations, they will turn the extravagant...praises which they are heaping upon me at this moment into equally extravagant...censures." Even further, Washington said that, "no event could have filled me with greater anxieties." It seems odd that a man who was about to take such an important post would say that, but at the same point, oddly refreshing. It was the other criminal who had the arrogance to think that he was in good standing with God, but the other criminal, the one who this book is about, who was humble enough to admit that he was, indeed, wrong.

In reading *Maxims of George Washington*, I learned of his Christian faith that is very different than the Christian faith that many of my Christian friends live out. Twice, he is mentioned in the book to be a Christian without ostentatiousness. Here are the two quotes below:

He had all the genuine mildness of Christianity, with all its force. He was neither ostentatiousness nor ashamed of his Christian profession.

Without making ostentatious professions of religion, he was a sincere believer in the Christian faith, and a truly devout man.

You may ask: what does it mean to be ostentatious when it comes to practicing Christianity? One of my pet peeves when I am out to eat with a fellow Christian is when he insists on being the one to bless the food. I don't have a problem with someone praying, but if you would like to have a blessing before the meal, always offer to have the other person bless the food. It shows that you believe that they are more holy than you, which shows humbleness. When my friend Tee Wamsley and I get together, he often does a quick silent prayer of five to ten seconds by himself. He doesn't want to seem even the least bit high and mighty by asking that we should, in fact, pray before a meal. Believe it or not, in my opinion, that is the style of faith which leads unbelievers to potentially pursue a relationship with Jesus Christ—or at least pique their interest a bit.

This is admissible as well. It is okay to talk about your faith with another person; the Bible of course encourages this, but tread carefully on how you approach the situation. I was having breakfast with an acquaintance one day in Atlanta. He was a hard partier in college but had since changed his ways in a rather big way. We had some nice small talk to begin, and then he immediately asked me, point blank, how my faith was. I immediately felt like he was the instructor, and I was his pupil. Needless to say, it didn't make me feel good at all. Compare that to how another one of my friends, Matt Lunati, handled the exact same situation. We hadn't talked in a while, and I told him I had just gone through a serious depression. We talked for a while and then Matt asked in the least ostentatious way, "I don't want to feel all high and mighty or super religious for asking this question, but how is your faith?"

One of my favorite reviews of my first book, *Forget Self-Help*, came from a man named John McKinnon, who hailed from the small South Georgia town of Douglas, GA. He coined the term "silent Christian," to describe someone whose actions spoke much louder than their words. In a quote that is wrongly attributed to St. Francis of Assisi, he says "Preach the Gospel at all times. Use words when necessary." The point of the quote is not that you shouldn't use words, after all, Romans 10:14 says: "how then will they call on Him in whom they have not believed? How will they believe in Him whom they have not heard? And how will they hear without a preacher?" It does, however, speak to *how* you should use them. I had been trying to get in touch with a friend's mother who I had left my first book with. I called her, texted her, did just about anything to get in touch with her. She finally called me back; we had a short conversation, and she just had to say "blessings" when she hung up the phone. What nerve she had, I thought to myself. We often wonder why people of other faiths are turned off by Christians; this is the reason why. If we were more like the criminal, and put our *actions* above our words, we would have much more success with bringing people to Christ.

One of my best friends growing up enlisted in the military a few years ago, specifically the Marines. He is probably the person I have talked to most frequently in the last few years over the phone. It's interesting; whenever I talk to him over the phone and ask him how is doing, he always responds the same way: "same old, same old." If I were doing the same things as he were doing, I probably wouldn't have that same humble nature. I find myself trying to promote when I do good far too much. I suppose it's the lack of security I have in myself.

He lives out the words in 1 Peter 5: 5-7 when it reads, "Young men, in the same way be submissive to those who are older. All of you, clothe yourselves with humility toward one another, because,

'God opposes the proud but gives grace to the humble.' Humble yourselves, therefore, under God's mighty hand, that he may lift you up in due time. Cast all your anxiety on him because he cares for you." It's amazing to think that it is often anxiety which forces us to be proud in the first place. I'm always the most arrogant when I don't feel secure with myself. When I am secure with myself, I don't boast. It's incredible what profound of an impact a small act he did could have on my own life.

When it comes to politics, my only rule is that you should never let your politics get in the way of helping people. I believe both parties are guilty of not living this simple suggestion out. I will say that one of the most powerful things I have heard a politician do is when George W. Bush refused to play golf again when he sent U.S. troops into Iraq. That action or inaction not to play golf while they were soldiers fighting in Iraq sent a message to the troops that Bush was not going to lead from behind, but from the side. That was the definition of leadership to me. While the Iraq war was not a popular one from the view of politicians from both sides of the aisle, that gesture showed Bush's character in full form.

Despite my first book's widespread media coverage, many of my friends still refused to read my book. Somebody I knew of took a different approach when he found out about my book. Believe it or not, I sold dozens of copies of my book at a Mexican restaurant in Northern Buckhead called Taxco. One night I was there with a date, and I immediately saw a man I recognized. I knew him because my sister Susie had played softball with his daughter at NYO and at Westminster. I had a good conversation the previous year with him at an event at Westminster. From the stories he was telling me, I could tell he was very successful. I would later learn that he has degrees from both MIT and Harvard and was a captain during the Airforce in the Vietnam area.

When I saw him, I re-introduced myself and told him and his wife that my book was selling in the restaurant we were in. What did he immediately do when I told him it was selling? He got up from his table and bought a book. I was stunned. A man who (had money) in Buckhead, to have money in Buckhead you have to be worth over $10 million dollars, got up and purchased a book of mine. His reaction to my book was the *complete opposite* of the majority of my mentors who if they did read the book, it took them months, and even then it seemed like it was a chore, and not an honor to support a mentee. In *The Purpose Driven Life*, Rick Warren says it best when he says "humbleness isn't thinking less of yourself, it's thinking of yourself less."

It also reminded of one of the most beautiful passages of the Bible entitled: "Imitating Christ's Humility" found in Philippians 2:1 – 2:13:

"Therefore if you have any encouragement from being united with Christ, if any comfort from his love, if any common sharing in the Spirit, if any tenderness and compassion, then make my joy complete by being like-minded, having the same love, being one in spirit and of one mind. Do nothing out of selfish ambition or vain conceit. Rather, in humility value others above yourselves, not looking to your own interests but each of you to the interests of the others.

In your relationships with one another, have the same mindset as Christ Jesus: Who, being in very nature God, did not consider equality with God something to be used to his own advantage; rather, he made himself nothing by taking the very nature of a servant, being made in human likeness. And being found in appearance as a man, he humbled himself by becoming obedient to death—even death on a cross! Therefore God exalted him to the highest place and gave him the name that is above every name, that at the name of Jesus every knee should bow, in heaven and on earth and under the earth, and every tongue acknowledge that Jesus Christ is Lord, to the glory of God the Father."

That's arguably the neatest part of Christianity to me. Jesus never seeks earthly might. To be a king is to be rich, powerful, carry a good name, and have lots of servants. I guess Jesus never got the memo. For him, power was in being *with* us, not *over* us. No other religion can claim that their deity acted in this way. In Matthew 20:16, Jesus says, "the last shall be first, and the first shall be last." It's the exact opposite of how we are taught to view life growing up in high school or university. It's not a novel concept, but I've noticed throughout life that you can tell someone's true character by how they treat people at the bottom of the totem pole. The reason for this is simple: they have nothing to gain by helping those out at the bottom. Expending energy when you're trying to help people lower than you is one of the most noble causes someone can take on. When I would play golf with my friend Tee Wamsley at Piedmont Driving Club,[7] I picked up on how his father, Tom, would treat the caddie masters that worked at the Club. He was gracious and would laugh and smile, treating him the exact same way he treated a millionaire buddy from Buckhead who belonged to the club.

---

[7] Out of all the country clubs in Atlanta, Piedmont Driving Club is perhaps the most storied and exclusive. Its in-town facility overlooks famed Piedmont Park and its beautiful golf course is located down by the airport.

In sizing up a potential son-in-law or daughter-in-law, the best way to see if they are going to be a good fit is to see how they treat people who are in a lesser position than them. Although your son or daughter may be madly in love now, at some point, they are going to be in the exact same position of that low person, and how they treated that low person in that particular situation is exactly how they will treat them. It's the associative property.[8]

I was lucky enough to lead a Bible Study with Westminster kids that went to my former church Peachtree Presbyterian in my early career. While I liked them all the same, there was one who I knew was going to be a great success by the *actions*, not *words*, he demonstrated during the time I spent with him. When we sold bottled water outside of Chastain Park amphitheater, he was by far the most tenacious one out there with an innate sense of how to treat the prospect that quite frankly, you can't teach. It wasn't surprising that when I saw him out on a date with a girl during the same time I saw the successful man, he went up and bought a copy of the book. This was even more impressive because I was no longer leading the Bible study at the time. When you allow yourself to be humble, you put yourself in a position to serve others that cannot be thwarted. Most people think that to be humble is the opposite of leading; they are wrong. If you have enough security in yourself to be humble you will not only lead but inspire others in a way you thought was never possible.

---

[8] In mathematics, the associative property is a property of some binary operations. In propositional logic, associativity is a valid rule of replacement for expressions in logical proofs. In layman's terms, you can replace things.

During the last few years, during my run-ins with truly impactful people such as Bill McDermott or [9]Eric Motley, I have sensed a change in them that is quite different than the people who are doing mundane things. I sense a humbleness in them that is without question the security they have in themselves. This humbleness is what allows for their leadership to change lives and create more people just like them. Most people are too proud to learn, but the most impactful of people always take the position that in order to impact people, you can never learn enough.

Flowers for Algernon has been a favorite book of mine for years. I read the book for the first time in 7th grade and have re-read it multiple times ever since. It is the most ironic book I have read, and in its irony, it reminds me often about how ironic Christianity is. Jesus is particularly ironic. In the Parable of the Workers in the Vineyard in Matthew 20: 1-16, irony ensues:

"For the kingdom of heaven is like a landowner who went out early in the morning to hire workers for his vineyard. He agreed to pay them a denarius for the day and sent them into his vineyard.

"About nine in the morning he went out and saw others standing in the marketplace doing nothing. He told them, 'You also go and work in my vineyard, and I will pay you whatever is right.' So they went.

"He went out again about noon and about three in the afternoon and did the same thing. About five in the afternoon he went

---

[9] Eric Motley and I are connected through the Sigma Chi chapter at Samford University. Motley served in the George W. Bush administration as Deputy Associate Director. He was the youngest appointee of the George W. Bush Administration at age 27. He currently serves as Executive Vice President and Corporate Secretary of the Aspen Institute.

out and found still others standing around. He asked them, 'Why have you been standing here all day long doing nothing?'

"'Because no one has hired us,' they answered.

"He said to them, 'You also go and work in my vineyard.'

"When evening came, the owner of the vineyard said to his foreman, 'Call the workers and pay them their wages, beginning with the last ones hired and going on to the first.'

"The workers who were hired about five in the afternoon came and each received a denarius. So when those came who were hired first, they expected to receive more. But each one of them also received a denarius. When they received it, they began to grumble against the landowner. 'These who were hired last worked only one hour,' they said, 'and you have made them equal to us who have borne the burden of the work and the heat of the day.'

"But he answered one of them, 'I am not being unfair to you, friend. Didn't you agree to work for a denarius? Take your pay and go. I want to give the one who was hired last the same as I gave you. Don't I have the right to do what I want with my own money? Or are you envious because I am generous?'

"So the last will be first, and the first will be last."

It doesn't seem right. It seems like the workers hired first should get more compensation. If we look through it through God's eyes, however, it makes complete sense, for we cannot do anything to earn salvation; that is only through believing in Christ. We're blessed in that when Jesus said, "It is finished," what it meant for us is that it was only getting started. Through his death on the cross, we could start to love again, start to matter again, but most of all, we could start to heal again. In healing again, we can start to live again. And we are doubly blessed in that most leaders close their doors. Most famous people try to avoid the paparazzi and fans. Not

Jesus though. He told us he would be with us until the end of the age.

The irony behind *Flowers for Algernon* is simple: Charlie, the main character is a retarded adult who wants to become smart like everyone else. He wants to be normal. He is constantly made fun of—even though he doesn't understand he is being made fun of—and, in general, is always a step behind. He finds it challenging to communicate with people in the way that normal people communicate with each other. A few doctors have a brilliant idea to use Charlie as an experiment to see if they can make retarded people smart. What Charlie didn't account for, however, is that he could become so smart that he would again have trouble communicating with people and living a normal life. At one point, Charlie says, "Am I a genius? I don't think so. Not yet anyway. As Burt would put it, mocking the euphemisms of educational jargon, I'm *exceptional*-a democratic term used to avoid the damning labels of *gifted* and *deprived* (which used to mean *bright* and *retarded*) and as soon as exceptional begins to mean anything to anyone they'll change it. The idea seems to be: use an expression only as long as it doesn't mean anything to anybody. *Exceptional* refers to both ends of the spectrum, so all my life I've been exceptional."

Often times, I confess that I, too, have felt like Charlie. The toughest part about having a mental illness is not necessarily what it does to you, but the stigma of it. The greatest part about going off to Samford after I had my manic episode is that nobody knew what had happened at Alabama; no one knew I was bipolar. The support system I had after the horrific event was good, at times. My family certainly supported me, and friends like Stuart Oglesby, John Solms, and Sheffield Hale came to visit me while I slowly got better. In the grade below, Tom Moak, William Bridges, and Ross Conway came to visit me as well, which was special. Still, there were others that were absent; they didn't make an effort to come.

It's interesting, in my favorite scene of *Flowers for Algernon*, Charlie goes to visit Warren, the institution that he will end up at when he is retarded again. During his visit, the warden, a Mr. Winslow, makes an interesting remark that has stuck with me for quite some time and will stick with me for the rest of my life. He says, "It's a good place. We have no psychiatrists on our staff—only an outside consulting man who comes in once every few weeks. But it's just as well. Everyone one of the psych staff is dedicated to his work. I couldn't have hired a psychiatrist, but at the price I'd have to pay I'm able to hire two psychologists—men who aren't afraid to give away a part of themselves to these people."

"What do you mean by 'a part of themselves'?"

"He studied me for a moment, and then through the tiredness flashed an anger. "There are a lot of people who will give money or materials, but very few who will give time and affection. That's what I mean." His voice grew harsh, and he pointed to an empty bottle on the bookshelf across the room.

"You see that bottle?"

I told him I had wondered about it when we came into his office.

"Well, how many people do you know who are prepared to take a grown man into his arms and let him nurse with the bottle? And take the chance of having the patient urinate or defecate all over him?"

A few times I have hand-written this quote to people I know going on mission trips. Their fervor for telling others about Jesus inspires me. Another time I sent the note on to someone was when I sent it on to Bill McDermott, CEO of SAP. We've developed a friendship over the last three years that started when I asked him for a job. I've kept him apprised of what I have been up to the last few years, and he always responds within hours, if not minutes. When I published *Forget Self-Help*, I expected to get a lot more support from my older male mentors than I actually ended up receiving. Despite the fact that I would wish these men a Happy Father's Day myself, none seemed to be interested in my book. There was one mentor who was different, however.[10] That was Bill McDermott. He was the second person to review my book on Amazon, and you better believe he read the whole thing considering he had to check every minute detail to make sure he could get behind a book. You also better believe he was busy himself, too; after all, he was managing 85,000 employees at the time.

---

[10] There was actually another mentor who read the book quickly and bought several copies. Ironically, his name is Bill, and he was also in sales. I am referring to Bill Dixon, who was both a mentor and professor of mine at Samford.

6

A "Dang" Mess

Only when we admit that we are a "dang" mess, are we capable of accepting the cross and receive God's grace. If you think you are anything short of that, you will fail to establish a relationship with him. This is the root of Christianity; it's certainly a different way to think about ourselves than what we are taught about in kindergarten and elementary school. There, teachings are all about self-esteem and the emphasis is based on self-care; this is no way to live, however, if someone wants to gain a close relationship with Christ. God knows you and knows your sin well.

In *A River Runs Through It,* Norman McClean writes, "all that a rod has to do is lift the line, the leader, and the fly is off the water, give them a good toss over the head, and then shoot them forward so they will land in the water without a splash in the following order: fly, transparent leader, and then the line—otherwise the fish will see the fly is a fake be gone."

In Romans 3:23, Paul writes, "for all have sinned and fall short of the glory of God." Just as McClean writes in a *River Runs Through It,* until we admit our sin, we are merely a fake to God. Not just a fake, but a phony. There is no character in American literature that despises phoniness more than Holden, the narrator and main character of *Catcher in the Rye*, by J.D. Salinger. He talks incessantly about them, always questioning their motives, always questioning their true purpose in life. Although this book has little to do with religion, there is no other book which outlines what we truly are as human beings. We are all fake, all lost, void of anything worthwhile without the blood of Jesus. We all need blood in order to survive. Why live only to survive, why not live to thrive? We can, but only with the blood of Jesus. Only his blood is pure, that is for sure. At one point in the novel, Holden goes on a rant about the Disciples: "Take the Disciples, for instance. They annoy the hell out of me, if you want to know the truth. They were all right after Jesus was dead and all, but while He was alive, they were about as much use to Him as a hole in the head. All they did was keep letting Him down." Holden is right. All we are just holes on the wall. What he doesn't realize, however, is we can become whole again once we accept Christ as our Lord and Savior. When we repent, we are secure. It's a security that is much more comforting than a 401K or a seat belt in a car. It's a security that transcends all understanding, and once you have it, all you want to do is pass it on. After all, to give that security is to give life. And it's not just life on this earth, it's life everlasting. Many times, throughout my life, I have not wanted to repent and have felt saddened by the need to do so. I want to be independent— to do things on my own. Living life this way has produced nothing but failure after failure, however. I need Jesus' blood just as I need oxygen, food, water, and shelter. Without it, I can never survive, never thrive. Without it I am a nobody; I can achieve nothing. With it, I am not only powerful, I am free.

Vulnerability is seen as a weakness in men. This is a real shame. We are taught to mask our feelings as men and if we don't, we risk being called what a man fears most: a woman. In *A Separate Peace*, by John Knowles, there are two best friends named Phineas and Gene at the prestigious Devon School in New England. Phineas, or Finny for short, is seen as the athletic good-looking jock while Gene is seen as the more studious nerd. Despite their differences, they are the best of friends. Finny has a way with people; he seems to get everything he wants. As the book goes on, the reader is able to decipher the jealousy that Gene has of Finny. Whatever Finny does, he succeeds at.

One day, Finny asks Gene to go to the beach. They both go and have a good time and end up spending the night at the beach. As they are going to bed, Finny quips, "I hope you're having a pretty good time here. I know I kind of dragged you away at the point of a gun, but after all you can't come by yourself, and at this teen-age period in life the proper person is your best pal." He hesitated and then added, "which is what you are," and there was silence on his dune.

It was a courageous thing to say. Exposing a sincere emotion nakedly like that at the Devon School was the next thing to suicide."

There's no question that when Knowles had this in mind, he outlined who was the stronger character. Finny was bold enough to say what he really meant; Gene was not. Expressing oneself at first is difficult, but over time it becomes easier and easier and something that we need to do in order to maintain true long-lasting relationships. It breaks down barriers and invites the other person to come back and meet you half-way.

*

One of the most poignant examples of a character admitting he is a dang mess and that he needs help is the movie, *Flight*. Denzel

Washington plays the role of Whip Whitaker, a talented pilot for Delta. Although he is talented, he is a severe alcoholic. During his last flight, he pulls off a miraculous landing, saving more than 100 passengers. Unfortunately, during that last flight he was also technically drunk, which causes complications for him legally later on. A failed marriage with a teenage son complicates matters, which flares up throughout the movie.

At one point in the movie, in a drunken rampage, Whip's son, Will, asks Whip, "who are you?" At that moment, Whip was nothing but a two-faced, lying scoundrel, who was a horrible father and husband. He was deceitful and weak—the opposite of a role model.

Later on, as Whip checks into the hotel, he holds a Coca-Cola. It was supposed to be his only drink that night; unfortunately, it was not. Although they took the alcohol at of his room, the door adjoining his was unlocked. One look at the other hotel room filled with Grey Goose, Sutter Home, Ketel One, Jose Cuervo, and others, and he cannot resist the urge to drink, and drink heavily. The next morning, Hugh and the air pilot come in and find the room in disarray and Whip passed out in the bathroom, all bloodied up from a drunken fall. When they do wake him up, he insists that he be "medically stimulated" with cocaine. When he is about to walk into the hearing, the air pilot gives him advice on how to answer certain questions about his drinking. Whip simply responds, "don't tell me how to lie about my drinking, okay I've been lying about my drinking my whole life."

Once Whip admits that he is in fact a drunk, a strange thing happens. Above, when he is with his son Will, I described him as deceitful and weak—the opposite of a role model. After he tells the truth, he is the opposite: he's honest and strong—the definition of a role model. His son later visits him in prison and is truly proud of him. He again asks the question, "who are you?" Instead of in a demeaning tone however, he asks in a proud, curious tone.

How do you walk in God's grace again? Are you courageous enough to be like Whip in this movie, or are you going to act like you don't have any flaws? Admit that you are weak, and then you become strong; it's that simple. In a world where we like to have complete control, this is a challenge.

At the end of the movie, in prison, Whip says,

That was it. I was finished. I was done. It was as if I had reached my lifelong limit of lies. I could not tell one more lie. And maybe I'm a sucker. Because if I had told just one more lie, I could've walked away from all that mess and kept my wings, kept my false sense of pride. And more importantly, I could've avoided being locked up in here with all you nice folks for the last thirteen months. But I'm here. And I'll be here for at least the next four or five years. And that's fair. I betrayed the public trust. I did. That's how the judge explained it to me. I had betrayed the public trust. The FAA, they took away my pilot's license. And that's fair. My chances of ever flying again are slim to none. And I accept that. I've had a lot of time to think about it, all of it. I've been doing some writing. I wrote letters to each of the families that had lost loved ones. Some of them were able to hear my apology. Some of them never will. I also apologized to all the people that tried to help me along the way, but I couldn't or wouldn't listen. People like my wife, you know. My ex-wife and, uh, my son. And again, like I said, you know, some of them will never forgive me. Some of them will. But at least I'm sober. I thank God for that. I'm grateful for that. And this is gonna sound real stupid coming from a man who's locked up in prison, but for the first time in my life, I'm free.

Rarely does one admit they're a dang mess because everyone's afraid of what people will think when they admit their faults. They're afraid of what negative thoughts people will associate with them. Little do they realize, however, that all the negativity washes away more quickly than it came because of the power repentance has. Repentance is the most out of the world action a human can do. We're often taught to present our best selves to the world even though deep down we know this is not for the best. The reason it is not for the best is clear: it is a lie; it is not true. We are all sinful; we all are in need of the cross to get that less-than-better self-transformed into our best self.

Repenting does not come easy, however, and it does not come easy for Captain Whitaker to admit that he was not only wrong, but that he endangered many lives on board because of his drinking habit. When he's in the hospital, he does have the wherewithal to refuse the alcohol that his friend brought him. Later on, Captain Whitaker goes into the stairwell for a smoke break. There, he runs into two other people, a beautiful woman who is in there for a heroin overdose, and a cancer patient who is about to die. They get into a theological discussion, and the cancer patient says, "death gives you perspective." For the criminal on the cross, it certainly did. The real question is, why can't we get this perspective before we are about to die? Why can't we live the way God wants us to live during the mundane, everyday moments of our lives? What are we afraid of? That which we are afraid of seems to have blinded us to the point of never coming back.

At the end of the novel, in *Catcher in the Rye*, Holden says, "Anyway, I keep picturing all these little kids playing some game in this big field of rye and all. Thousands of little kids, and nobody's around - nobody big, I mean - except me. And I'm standing on the edge of some crazy cliff. What I have to do, I have to catch everybody if they start to go over the cliff - I mean if they're running and they don't look where they're going I have to come out from somewhere and catch them. That's all I do all day. I'd just be the catcher in the rye and all. I know it's crazy, but that's the only thing I'd really like to be."

Just like Holden, all Jesus is to us is a catcher in the rye. He can only play that role, however, if we repent. Just like Holden, Jesus tells us, "that's all I do all day." For me, the first feeling I think of when I realize this is disbelief; the second one is utter relief. Permanent relief though, has an effect that temporary relief cannot have on you: permanent relief is worry free, the type of relief a child experiences when he jumps into his parent's bed after a bad dream, or the type of relief that a big white oak provides in the South during a hot summer day. Or it could be a bench[11]. Whatever it is, permanent relief will never let you down. In its permanence, it gives you a strength that cannot be unbroken.

A Little Guilt Goes a Long Way

One of the biggest lies that the devil throws at us is that feeling guilty about something we did is a sin. This couldn't be further from the truth, however. Guilt in small doses is good for us and helps us to repent from our sin. Have you ever done something you said you

---

[11] See cover of *Forget Self-Help* to understand this reference

weren't going to do but did it anyway and felt guilty about? You might have even done it over and over again even though you promised yourself that you would never do it. Slowly but surely, you feel less and less guilty until it becomes engrained in your normal conduct, and you never feel guilty again. You not feeling guilty is not a product of Jesus' grace, but instead it is the devil leading you down his treacherous path.

You can tell how much someone believes in the cross by how open they are about their own sin. I have many devout Christian friends. I've noticed that, oftentimes, the more devout they are, the less likely they are to admit the extent to which they sin. One would think that this would be the opposite because they supposedly have a strong relationship with Christ. I have, rarely, if ever found that to be the case. One exception of this came when I was in high school and had a good friend on the golf team. He opened up about his sin to all of us. He struggled with lust and pride—I don't blame him for that because he was a really good golfer—and he was open about it. In doing so, he was like the criminal on the cross. He was open and vulnerable, which is how God wants us to be. As long as we are like that, we can become like Him.

A great passage in The Bible that explains just this can be found in 2 Corinthians 8-11. Paul writes, "Even if I caused you sorrow by my letter, I do not regret it. Though I did regret it—I see that my letter hurt you, but only for a little while—yet now I am happy, not because you made me sorry, but because your sorrow lead to repentance. For you became sorrowful as God intended and so were not harmed in any way by us. Godly sorrow brings repentance that leads to salvation and leaves no regret, but worldly sorrow brings death. See what this godly sorrow has produced in you: what earnestness, what eagerness to clear yourselves, what indignation, what alarm, what longing, what concern, what readiness to see justice done." We should never have prolonged periods of grief, but when you feel guilty after you sin, it means you are becoming more Christ-like. It means that your wants and desires are becoming His wants and desires. George Washington once said, "Labor to keep alive in your breast that little spark of celestial fire called conscience." It is true, you cannot earn your way into God's graces, but at the same point, you should strive to be able to look yourself in the mirror each and every day.

Accepting Help

One of the humblest acts a person can do actually isn't about doing anything at all, it's about having something done to them: accepting help. For me, accepting help from an early age wasn't about being humble, it was a necessity to make sure I passed all my courses at Westminster. I would be a regular at "extra-help" in courses such as English, Math, Science, Spanish, and just about every course I ever took there. I was used to failing in class, so I got used to accepting help.

So many of my friends refuse to accept any help I offer, any advice I give. One of my favorite complements that I got on my Amazon reviews for *Forget Self-Help* was when Bill McDermott said I was a "life long-learner." Along those same lines, Robert E. Lee might have put it best when he said that, "the education of a man is never completed until he dies." The humility that he shows in that statement is earth-shattering. What if our politicians today thought this way? In *The Road to Character*, David Brooks said, "We don't become better because we acquire new information. We become better because we acquire better loves. We don't become what we know. Education is a process of love formation. When you go to a school, it should offer you new things to love." To me, the most pronounced time this happened is when my history teacher, Mr. Tribble, suggested I read *Uncle Tom's Cabin* by Harriet Beecher Stowe in 10th grade. It's quite a long book, and l enjoyed it enough that I would eventually write a book about it. I once completed an essay of his before he even technically assigned it. Not to be outdone, I voluntarily read some Amy Tan in another English teacher's class. I have never gotten enough of learning, and I have tried to remember that I have "never arrived" at the end goal. Learning how to be more Christlike is something to always strive for. If you have a humble view of yourself, you will always be enticed to learn more.

In a *River Runs Through It,* Neal often wonders if he can help his brother, Paul, who is a severe alcoholic with a gambling problem. When he discusses the issue with his Dad, his Dad gives him such sage words. He tells him: "Help, is giving part of yourself to somebody who comes to accept willingly and needs it badly."

"So it is, that we can seldom help anybody. Either we don't know what part to give or maybe we don't like to give any part of ourselves. Then, more often than not, the part that is needed is not wanted."

I have been in this situation many times with friends as well as family members. The most telling review that I got from my book *Forget Self Help* is when a reviewer from a small town in Arkansas simply said that "the most important part will be getting this book into the hands of people who need to read it." I've noticed that the more selfless and genuine a person is, the more they have appreciated the book. I noticed that some new-age Christians took issue with the book because it was too much about unselfishness (Jesus' actions) vs. what He did for us on the cross. I soon came to realize that my book did not have the power to turn a selfish person into an unselfish person. Did it have the power to turn a person who is pretty unselfish into a person who was even more unselfish? Why, yes. But it was sad when I realized that a selfish person would not want to read it, and because of this, I realized they would never enjoy the happiness of living a truly unselfish life. I have found a quote misattributed to Winston Churchill to be spot on when he supposedly said, "You make a living by what you get, you make a life by what you give."

Although I am all about courage, there is sometimes a time and place where you have to cut your losses and stop trying to help someone out. Too much time and effort can be wasted. Most importantly, you could be trying to help someone else out. It's not the same as the parable of the lost sheep because there are many more sheep out there that are lost, not just one.

7

What Are You Chasing After?

During the last 5 years, I have often chased after things that I thought would bring me ultimate pleasure. Early on in my career it seemed to be chasing after a romantic relationship. Later on, it was money and status. Now, it seems like the thing I chase after most is accomplishment. In *Counterfeit Gods: The Empty Promises of Money, Sex, and Power, and the Only Hope that Matters*, Tim Keller lays out a real sense of what humans are really after. On the back cover of the book, he is quite clear about what that is. He writes, "Success, money, true love, and the life you've always wanted. Many of us place our faith in these things, believing they held the key to happiness, but with a sneaking suspicion they might not deliver. No wonder we feel lost, alone, disenchanted, and resentful. There is only one God who can wholly satisfy our cravings—and now is the perfect time to meet Him again, or for the first time."

For me, the longing for money really began when I was 24. I was given my projected earnings after a raise, and, for a 24-year-old, it was really quite high. I made quite a bit of money in a job after that, and if a few deals closed in my next job, I was convinced that I could potentially make 7-figures in one year as a 26-year-old. When those deals didn't close, I was beyond disappointed and fell into the deepest depression of my life. It didn't help that I was engulfed in the Buckhead scene, a scene that rewards money, success, and power. In *Flowers for Algernon*, Charlie believes that once he becomes smart, he will be accepted. At one point, in the process of him becoming smart, he says, "What do smart pepul think about or remember. Fancy things I bet. I wish I knew some fancy things alredy." I had the pleasure of having bible study with a then 30-something-year-old who grew up in a similar socio-economic background to us and had a job we could easily have 20 years down the line. He went to rival high school Lovett and worked in commercial real-estate, a very typical job for someone in Buckhead to have. One of the things that I remember Brett saying is that it was a never-ending cycle among his friends to see how much money they were making. He said that once someone hit $100,000, they would go for $200,000. Then later once someone hit $300,000, they would go for $500,000. Ambition is a good thing in itself, but once it begins to replace striving after Godly things in one's life, it can be destructive. When you find yourself obsessing over one thing, you must ask yourself: is the reason I am so focused on this thing for my own personal gain, or is it because it will advance the gospel? That's ultimately the check point we should ask ourselves when we become ambitious.

Charlie believes that once he becomes smart, all of his problems would vanish. What he didn't realize would happen, however, is that once he became smart, all of his problems did not only not vanish, they got worse. Miss Kinnian, Charlie's teacher, tells Charlie that (his intelligence will come slowly) "and you have to werk very hard to get smart." Luckily, this is not how it works in getting into a relationship with Jesus Christ. After all, Tim Keller, said in *Counterfeit*

Gods that "God's salvation does not come in response to a changed life. A changed life comes in response to the salvation, offered as a free gift." Immediately, when we tell him we are a sinner, he meets us with his grace.

I've read *Flowers for Algernon* multiple times. The most beautiful aspect in Keyes writing is his ability to show Charlie's progression in intelligence through his journal entries. It is gradual, gradual in the way a golf ball on a green curves around with each undulation, or to put it more simply, gradual in the way you see a young boy grow into full-grown man in what seems to be in the blink of an eye to his parents. In my most recent reading of the book—or in this case, a speed reading—the first time I noticed when Charlie was getting smarter was when he used an em dash. I just used one in the previous sentence. According to thepunctuation.com, "the em dash is perhaps the most versatile punctuation mark. Depending on the context, the em dash can take the place of commas, parentheses, or colons—in each case to slightly different effect. Notwithstanding its versatility, the em dash is best limited to two appearances per sentence. The em dash makes our writing more clear and concise when we use it." William Pressly, the founder of my school, once said that, "rules hinder creativity at first, but once a set of simple punctuation rules becomes second nature, it ceases to be a hindrance. In fact, these kinds of restrictions can enhance creativity. After all, some of the most sensitive poetry in English was written in one of the strictest forms: the sonnet." Luckily for us however, the only "rule" we need to remember is just how weak we are by ourselves and how strong we can become with God through accepting his Son.

When pop-artist Taylor Swift came out with "Our Song" in 2009, she got nearly every tween girl, teenager[12] and others to fall in love with her. How could you not with her sweet voice, good looks, and timid, but genuine disposition.[13] Getting back to "Our Song," though. In the song, Taylor misses the point—completely. She asks her boyfriend over and over what her song is, and instead of naming an actual song, he names *actions* that they do together.

Actions have a way of speaking louder than words because they require a greater expenditure of energy than mere words. In *Uncle Tom's Cabin,* by Harriet Beecher Stowe, there is a kind master named St. Claire that said that he would eventually make out free papers for Tom. He never did so, and because of that, Tom was sold to a very hard master named Legree. When we fail to do the necessary actions that the criminal did, we lose out on what we can become. What the world sees as weak, God often sees as strong. So many times, I myself have tried to appear to others as strong, and, in doing so, have appeared as weak as ever. A prominent example of when a man humbled himself, and in doing so, made himself strong is an interaction that my father had with our rival high school's headmaster, Billy Peebles. My father had attended a college night at Lovett and had written a letter to Peebles, thanking him for hosting him that night. How did Peebles respond? He wrote a letter back to my father, thanking him for coming. Just like that, what many would consider too much of a chore to do, Peebles did it, and in doing so, showed his leadership ability just like the criminal. Leaders get down in the trenches; they do the dirty work. In the same vein, that's why

---

[12] , myself

[13] I admit, I have a small crush on her to this day and even sent her a letter with some pictures of me asking her out to dinner in Nashville three years ago. She never responded; I was crushed.

we can put so much trust in Jesus. He spent time on this earth going through heartache and ridicule just for us. Additionally, he laid down his life for us in a gruesome way. In many ways, the criminal and Jesus are one in the same, always pushing ahead, never looking back. The phrase that both of them play is the toughest phrase for us to do: self-sacrifice.

8

Gracias

Gratitude came naturally to me from an early age, which was a bit strange, considering I grew up the 9th wealthiest zip code in the nation, 30327. With all the money we were around, child-rearing was different in Buckhead. It was different in the sense that when you have so much wealth around you, it can be a challenge to insert the discipline necessary for children to have productive lives. Don't get me wrong, the majority of my friends are very successful today, but many of them don't possess the depth of gratitude that I developed from an early age. I don't know exactly the time when I started to pray that prayer I still pray today; I want to say it was around Junior High and high school. The prayer I prayed to God was simple: "God, you have given me so much, what can I give back to you?" I understood before every single one of my peers that I came from wealth, had a good access to superb education, and, for the most part, had a supportive family behind me. The one person I owe that appreciation is probably my mother, who refused that I become like everyone else on the block. She urged us to write thank-you notes and thank her and my father for meals out. When I went over to friends' houses for dinner, the parents of the friend who I went out to dinner were probably surprised that I even said thanks.

Eric Motley puts it best his memoir, *Madison Park: A Place of Hope*, when he says, "Blessings come at us so relentlessly; we are forever in a deficit position. We never get all of the thank-yous or goodbyes properly said, which leaves, each one, living with a burden of gratitude."

In the same vein, when I was a camp counselor at Camp Laney in Mentone, AL, I used this same style of thinking when any of my boys were homesick. Whenever any of my campers were homesick, I would encourage them to be thankful that they were homesick. It must mean that they have great, loving parents. I would encourage them to remember that not all children were as lucky as they were.

James 1: 2-4 says, "Consider it pure joy, my brothers, whenever you face trials of many kinds, because you know that the testing of your faith develops perseverance. Perseverance must finish its work so that you may be mature and complete, not lacking anything." It is tough to go through trials, but without them, we cannot be made strong. When I was in 10th grade, I quit basketball to focus on my golf game after my History teacher, Mr. Tribble, encouraged us to be a master on one, instead of a jack of all trades. When I started to focus solely on golf, a strange thing happened, I actually got worse. I had a case of the shanks[14]; it was not pretty. Eventually, though, it led me to take lessons and I got much better, better than I was ever before. Months later, in a tournament, I would actually

---

[14] A shank is a shot in golf where the ball is hit off the hozzle of the club face which forces to ball to go in a 60-degree angle to the left or right depending on whether the golfer is left-handed or right-handed. It is as demoralizing as a basketball player air-balling a free-throw.

shoot a 30 on nine holes in a competition. None of this would have happened if I hadn't struggled to begin with.

The '90's were certainly a good decade for music. One of my favorite songs was "Kind and Generous" by Natalie Merchant. Christ has been so kind and generous to give us his life to pay the debt for our sins. Out of respect for his deed, we should break through all the sin that so entangles our life and live for him. We do not do good out of duty, but out of His love for us. We could have never of come as far as we have without Him, but in Him, our opportunities are endless. Do I have trouble remembering this as much as I should? Absolutely! If this happens to you as it often does for me, crank up YouTube, search for this Natalie Merchant song called "Kind and Generous," and thank God for life through his Son. The criminal certainly did. In a 2005 VH1 Live show, Merchant told the attentive crowd, "I'm proud of this song because I wanted I always wanted to write a song that had a(n) extremely universal simple sentiment and, uh, just gratitude, that's all this song is about, and, uh, (I) really feel I accomplished my mission: simple, to the point and everyone knows what I'm talking about the first time they hear this song, and they can see along, so, sing along if you feel like it."

Natalie, while I did sing in the Alto section of the chorus in 6th grade at Westminster, you don't want to hear me sing period, much less a song about thankfulness; so, instead I'll write about it…

Thankfulness shouldn't be situation-based because difficult times have a way of shaping us in a stronger, more effective way than a seemingly encouraging time. It's more challenging to grow when things are going well. When you're at the very bottom, upward is the only direction you can go. To be thankful isn't to walk around with a smile on your face all the time. Jesus didn't have a smile on his face when he was crucified. After all, didn't he cry out, "why have you forsaken me?" He did have the wherewithal to trust God during that time, however. When you trust in God during the toughest of times, He credits that as thankfulness. For me, gratitude can frame meaningless drudgery into meaningful opportunities. When I look back on my life, I find myself more thankful for the strife that I went through than for the supposed good times. As simple as the following advice was, it is perhaps the most meaningful advice I have ever gotten in my life. McDermott encouraged me to focus on the journey, not the destination. The journey is hard, but in its difficulty, there lies the most opportunity to grow. This is important because this growth will enable you get through even more treacherous times ahead.

One of my favorite examples of gratitude occurring in American Literature is in the courtroom scene in *To Kill a Mockingbird*. In the book, Atticus Finch is charged to defend a black man in rural Alabama who is falsely accused of raping a white woman. Although Atticus comes up short and loses the case, the jury deliberated much longer than people would have thought considering the town was so racist. In many ways, it was a win for the black people of the town. When Atticus is leaving the court room, all the black people get up to stand as a gesture of thanks to him. Reverend Sykes has to wake up Scout and simply says, "Scout, stand up, your father's passing." We all have people like Atticus in our lives that are there for us constantly; we can never thank them enough.

9

The D Word

Disciple is the root word of discipline. So why is discipline seen as an *extremely* negative word and disciple as an extremely *positive* word? I'm going to say that again... Disciple is the root word of discipline. So why is discipline seen as an *extremely* negative word and disciple as an extremely *positive* word?

Disciple is the root word of discipline. So why is discipline seen as an *extremely* negative word and disciple as an extremely *positive* word? I'm going to say that again... Disciple is the root word of discipline. So why is discipline seen as an *extremely* negative word and disciple as an extremely *positive* word?

Disciple is the root word of discipline. So why is discipline seen as an *extremely* negative word and disciple as an extremely *positive* word? I'm going to say that again... Disciple is the root word of discipline. So why is discipline seen as an *extremely* negative word and disciple as an extremely *positive* word?

Disciple is the root word of discipline. So why is discipline seen as an *extremely* negative word and disciple as an extremely *positive* word? I'm going to say that again... Disciple is the root word of discipline. So why is discipline seen as an *extremely* negative word and disciple as an extremely *positive* word?

Disciple is the root word of discipline. So why is discipline seen as an *extremely* negative word and disciple as an extremely *positive* word? I'm going to say that again... Disciple is the root word of discipline. So why is discipline seen as an *extremely* negative word and disciple as an extremely *positive* word?

Disciple is the root word of discipline. So why is discipline seen as an *extremely* negative word and disciple as an extremely *positive* word? I'm going to say that again... Disciple is the root word of discipline. So why is discipline seen as an *extremely* negative word and disciple as an extremely *positive* word?

Disciple is the root word of discipline. So why is discipline seen as an *extremely* negative word and disciple as an extremely *positive* word? I'm going to say that again... Disciple is the root word of discipline. So why is discipline seen as an *extremely* negative word and disciple as an extremely *positive* word?

Disciple is the root word of discipline. So why is discipline seen as an *extremely* negative word and disciple as an extremely *positive* word? I'm going to say that again... Disciple is the root word of discipline. So why is discipline seen as an *extremely* negative word and disciple as an extremely *positive* word?

Disciple is the root word of discipline. So why is discipline seen as an *extremely* negative word and disciple as an extremely *positive* word? I'm going to say that again... Disciple is the root word of discipline. So why is discipline seen as an *extremely* negative word and disciple as an extremely *positive* word?

Disciple is the root word of discipline. So why is discipline seen as an *extremely* negative word and disciple as an extremely *positive* word? I'm going to say that again... Disciple is the root word of discipline. So why is discipline seen as an *extremely* negative word and disciple as an extremely *positive* word?

Sorry for the redundancy, but for the past few years, I've wondered how that could be the case. What do Christians, Jews, Hindus, Agnostics, Atheists and devil worshippers have in common? They seem to all *detest* being disciplined. From the people I've run into, including myself, it makes us feel small, or, less than perfect. There is no bigger blow to my ego than to receive discipline or criticism. To this *day*, I have *never* had someone openly thank me for disciplining them *except* for one friend, Tee Wamsley. He's certainly an outlier, and I almost wish he hadn't acted like the criminal because I expect others to do the same. It might seem like a paradox, but you want to try to be a person that no one wants to be around because when he leaves your presence they are immediately disappointed by the decreased level of character and encouragement they are now forced to be around in terms of dealing with other people.

With that being said, there is a *right* way to impart discipline, and there is a *wrong* way to impart discipline. I am probably the chief example of how to impart discipline the wrong way. I often shame the person, instead of trying to build them up. This is no good because it shows that I am not trying to help the person become, necessarily. I may even be trying to build myself up in the process. If you are too easy on the person, however, you won't see any change. One of my favorite professors at Samford was known for literally staring down a person if they were late to class. As mean as this seemed to the person, it was quite effective. Many people knew not to be late to Dr. Marshall's class after that.

One of the strongest predictors of success a person will have in their future life is how they respond to discipline. Are they defensive? The answer is probably so, at least, at first. Do they have enough sense to appreciate where the other person is coming from? If they are this type of person, I guarantee they will be a success. Admitting you're wrong, just the like the criminal did, will certainly ensure a more successful life and give you the ability to influence others more easily. You will be first, just as the criminal was the first convert.

I personally love it when people give me criticism; it makes me become a better person. Actually, a few years ago, the first time I met with my boss at one of the start-ups I worked at, I only had one request: if I was doing anything that wasn't to the ability he thought I should be doing, to tell me immediately. I can also remember another ex-girlfriend telling me I made poor eye-contact. At first, I wasn't too happy, and then I took it as a learning experience and thanked her multiple times for telling me of my weakness. It's in these simple moments where we learn the most. If she hadn't said anything, it would have showed that she thought I was not capable of change. I challenge the people I respect, but to those who have neither the capacity nor ability to change, I am silent. The Lord agrees. In what is probably my favorite passage in all of the Bible, Hebrews 12:4 – 13 states:

In your struggle against sin, you have not yet resisted to the point of shedding your blood. And have you completely forgotten this word of encouragement that addresses you as a father addresses his son? It says,

"My son, do not make light of the Lord's discipline, and do not lose heart when he rebukes you, because the Lord disciplines the one he loves, and he chastens everyone he accepts as his son."

Endure hardship as discipline; God is treating you as his children. For what children are not disciplined by their father? If you are not disciplined—and everyone undergoes discipline—then you are not legitimate, not true sons and daughters at all. Moreover, we have all had human fathers who disciplined us and we respected them for it. How much more should we submit to the Father of spirits and live! They disciplined us for a little while as they thought best; but God disciplines us for our good, in order that we may share in his holiness. No discipline seems pleasant at the time, but painful. Later on, however, it produces a harvest of righteousness and peace for those who have been trained by it.

Therefore, strengthen your feeble arms and weak knees. "Make level paths for your feet," so that the lame may not be disabled, but rather healed.

It is true that you should not judge others; after all, in Matthew 7:1-5, Jesus urges us not to do so. He tells us, "do not judge, or you too will be judged. For in the same way you judge others, you to will be judged, and with the measure you use, it will be measured to you. Why do you look at the speck of sawdust in your brother's eye and pay no attention to the plank in your own eye? How can you say to your brother, 'let me take the speck out of your eye,' when all the time there is a plank in your own eye? You hypocrite, first take the plank out of your own eye, and then you will see clearly to remove the speck from your brother's eye." When approaching one another in situations like these, we must follow Micah 6:8's admonishment to walk towards one another "with justice and mercy." We need to make sure that we are not all high and mighty when trying to correct one another's actions, but at the same point, the Bible tells us in Proverbs 27:17 that as men and women, we must sharpen one another. Robert E. Lee put it best when he said, "a true man of honor feels humbled himself when he cannot help humbling others." I should put these words into action more often.

I've gotten a few traffic tickets the last few years, and each time I have gotten one, I've ended up in the honorable Christopher Ward's courtroom in downtown Atlanta. I've never been in such a place; his courtroom is the definition of law and order. Every few hours, he proudly announces that his courtroom takes the most cases in the South, and he plans to keep it that way. There is no talking allowed, no cell phone usage allowed, and most of all, no sleeping. Pants are to be worn all the way up as well. While most people are probably annoyed by the rules, I found a refreshing sense about them. I suppose he was doing it for our own benefit. Think about this: when you are at a left-hand turn light and find yourself looking down on the phone and you hear a honk behind you telling you to go, at first you are startled, maybe even annoyed. Then, however, you are happy because you get to go towards your destination. That is what God is doing to us when he disciplines us: he is just sending us to our destination in a more expedient way than if we had been left on our way to get there.

Conclusion

She rattled the ice in my plastic cup
I said "yes m'am", fill her up
Tell me something good that I don't know
'Cause this world's been kicking my behind
Life ain't been a friend of mine
Lately I've been feeling kinda low
And she looked back over her shoulder
Pointed at the sign hanging up on the wall
It said
Everything's gonna be alright
Everything's gonna be alright
And nobody's gotta worry 'bout nothing
Don't go hittin' that panic button[15]

We all have that sign when we become vulnerable, adhere to the highest standards of integrity, show gratitude, and strive to be courageous. We have to do these things to repent, every single one of

---

[15] "Everything's Going to Be Alright" by David Lee Murphy and Kenny Chesney

them. When we don't, we are simply a wretch. The criminal serves as a guide to us all. He's humble, yet unafraid, clever without the usual pretentiousness, but most of all, he is loyal, and in his loyalty, he became the first convert to Christianity; in doing so, he joined Jesus in paradise forever.

AUTHOR'S NOTE

There are intentional misspellings in some of the parts dealing with *Flowers for Algernon* by Daniel Keyes.

I suppose the reason that I decided to write such a book about the criminal on the cross is that I really relate to him, for I am a sinner— a frequent one at that. I needed a way out; I needed a Savior.

REFERENCES

Introduction

1. http://www.rutgersprep.org/ken-dall/books/what_the_dog_saw.html "Notes on *What the Dog Saw* by Malcom Gladwell." 8-6-2012

Chapter 1

1. *Holy Bible*. NIV. 1986. Zondervan. Grand Rapids, Michigan. Luke 23: 40-43 p. 1641.
2. "The Fringe benefits of failure, and the importance of imagination." https://news.harvard.edu/ga-zette/story/2008/06/text-of-j-k-rowling-speech/ June 5, 2008.
3. "Learning to Allow temporary failure: potential benefits, supportive practices and teacher concern" https://www.tandfonline.com/doi/abs/10.1080/0260747032000162299 Volume 30, 2004, Issue 1.
4. "Gold-Digger." Kanye West https://genius.com/Kanye-west-gold-digger-lyrics 3-23-2019.
5. Rosalyn Carter Quotes. https://www.amazon.com/must-accept-that-might-fail/dp/B01LYTDB8S 3-23-2019.
6. Martin Luther King Jr. Quotes. http://the-kingcenter.org/blog/mlk-quote-week-times-challenge-and-controversy 3-23-2019.
7. *David and Goliath*. Malcom Gladwell. p.148. Back Bay Books. 2013.

8. Michael Jordan Quotes. https://www.shmoop.com/quotes/failed-why-i-suc-ceed.html 3-23-2019.
9. "No Tears Left to Cry" by Ariana Grande. https://genius.com/Ariana-grande-no-tears-left-to-cry-lyrics 3-23-2019.
10. "Try Again." https://genius.com/Aaliyah-try-again-lyrics 3-23-2019.
11. Proverbs 24:10. Page 1020.
12. Ronald Reagan Quotes. https://www.nationalarchivesstore.org/products/it-can-be-done-ronald-reagan-plaque 3-23-2019.
13. Amy Tan. *Joy Luck Club*. Penguin Books. 2006. Page 58.
14. "Jack Nicklaus to Jordan Speith: Chin up, young man." Matt Bonesteel. April 11, 2016. https://www.washingtonpost.com/news/early-lead/wp/2016/04/11/jack-nicklaus-to-jordan-spieth-chin-up-young-man/?noredirect=on&utm_term=.156249f38d3b
15. Bobby Jones call penalty on himself at 1925 US Open. https://www.golf.com/tour-and-news/bobby-jones-calls-penalty-himself-1925-us-open October 19, 2015.
16. "This one's going to hurt a while." Jim Litke. https://www.nwaonline.com/news/2016/apr/11/this-one-s-going-hurt-a-while-20160411/ April 11th, 2016.
17. "I'm Real." Jennifer Lopez. https://genius.com/Jennifer-lopez-im-real-murder-remix-lyrics 3-23-2019.
18. *Flowers for Algernon*. Daniel Keyes. Mariner Books. Page 1.
19. *Flowers for Algernon*. Daniel Keyes. Mariner Books. Page 27.

20. "Learning to Fly." Tom Petty and the Heartbreakers." https://genius.com/Tom-petty-and-the-heartbreakers-learning-to-fly-lyrics 3-23-2019.
21. *Robert E. Lee: a Biography*. Emory Thomas. W.W. Norton. page 19.
22. Jeremiah 29:11. page 1221.
23. MLK Quotes. http://thekingcenter.org/blog/mlk-quote-week-faith-taking-first-step 3-23-2019
24. Recollection and Letters. Robert E. Lee. P. 221. 2004. Barnes & Noble publishing.
25. Luke 8:16. p.1606.

Chapter 2

1. Amy Tan. *Joy Luck Club*. Page 82-83.
2. Matthew 28: 28-30. p.1514.
3. "Pantala Naga Pampa." Dave Matthews Band. https://www.azlyrics.com/lyrics/davematthewsband/pantalanagapampa.html 3-23-2019.
4. Matthew 6:25-34 p.1504.
5. Thomas. page 80.
6. "Locked Up" Akon. https://genius.com/Akon-locked-up-lyrics 3-23-2019
7. *Counterfeit Gods*. Tim Keller. Page 19. Penguin 2011.
8. Amy Tan. *Joy Luck Club*. Page 207.
9. Mark 4:22. p. 1557.
10. Amy Tan. *Joy Luck Club*. Page 100.
11. Amy Tan. *Joy Luck Club*. Page 24-25.
12. *A River Runs Through It*. Norman McClean. The University of Chicago Press. page 2.

Chapter 3

1. *A Separate Peace.* John Knowles. Simon and Schuster. 2003. page 29.
2. Luke 23:46. Page 1641
3. *Daring Greatly: How the Courage to be Vulnerable Transforms the Way We Live.* Avery. 2015. Page 37.
4. *To Kill a Mockingbird.* Harper Lee. Perennial. 2002. Page 87.
5. *P.S. I love you.* Jackson Brown. Rutledge Hill 1991.
6. *13 Reasons Why.* Brian Yorkey. Netflix.
7. *He's Just Not That Into You.* Flower Films. 2009.
8. Luke 6:23. Page 1601.
9. "Amazing Grace." John Newton. 1779.
10. *The Big Short.* Paramount Pictures. 2015.

Chapter 4

1. "Promoting a Culture of Academic Integrity." Peggy Piascik and Gayle Brazeau. *American Journal of Pharmaceutical Education.* 2010 Aug 10. 74(6): 113.
2. "Eulogy of Henry Clay." *Illinois State Journal.* Delivered July 16th, 1852.
3. *The Making of Robert E. Lee.* Michael Fellman. Johns Hopkins University Press. 2003. Page 40.
4. *Emperor's Club.* Michael Hoffman. Universal Pictures. 2002.
5. "Man in the Mirror." Michael Jackson. https://www.azlyrics.com/lyrics/michaeljackson/maninthemirror.html 3-24-2019.
6. *Flight.* Paramount Pictures. 2012.

7. *What Every Man Wishes His Father Had Told Him.* Byron Forest Yawn. Harvest House Publishers. 2012.

8. "To be brave: be bold, be real, believe." Bill McDermott. May 8th, 2015. https://www.linkedin.com/pulse/brave-bold-real-believe-bill-mcdermott/.

9. "George Washington to Alexander Hamilton." August 28th, 1788. https://www.mountvernon.org/library/digi-talhistory/quotes/article/still-i-hope-i-shall-always-pos-sess-firmness-and-virtue-enough-to-maintain-what-i-con-sider-the-most-enviable-of-all-titles-the-character-of-an-honest-man/ 3-24-2019.

10. Proverbs 24:26. Page 1021.

11. "Drops of Jupiter." Train. https://www.azlyrics.com/lyr-ics/train/dropsofjupiter.html 3-24-2019.

12. *A Separate Peace.* John Knowles. Simon and Schuster. 2003. pages 69-70.

Chapter 5

1. Proverbs 31:30. Page 1033.

2. Matthew 18:1-5. Page 1526.

3. *Lincoln's Melancholy: How Depression Challenged a President and Fueled His Greatness.* Joshua Wood Shenk. Mariner Books. 2005. Page 179.

4. Kenneth Blanchard. Quotes from goodreads.com https://www.goodreads.com/quotes/56863-none-of-us-is-as-smart-as-all-of-us 3-24-2019.

5. "Q & A with David Bob." December 23, 2013. C-SPAN. https://www.c-span.org/video/?316911-1/qa-david-bobb&desktop=.

6. Matthew 8: 5-13. Page 1507.
7. "George Washington: The Reluctant President." Ron Chernow. Smithsonian Magazine. February 2011. https://www.smithsonianmag.com/history/george-washington-the-reluctant-president-49492/.
8. *Maxims of George Washington*. The Mount Vernon Ladies Association. Pages 199 and 202.
9. "FactChecker: Misquoting Francis of Assisi."Glenn Stanton July 10, 2012. https://www.thegospelcoalition.org/article/factchecker-misquoting-francis-of-assisi/
10. Romans 10:14. Page 1761.
11. 1 Peter 5: 5-7. Page 1892.
12. *Purpose-Driven Life*. Rick Warren. Zondervan 2002.
13. Philippians 2: 2-11. Page 1827.
14. Matthew 20:16. Page 1530.
15. Matthew 20: 1-16. Page 1530.
16. *Flowers for Algernon*. Daniel Keyes. Mariner Books. Page 153
17. *Flowers for Algernon*. Daniel Keyes. Mariner Books. Page 230.

Chapter 6

1. *A River Runs Through It*. Norman McClean. The University of Chicago Press. page 2.
2. Romans 3:23. Page 1751.
3. *Catcher in the Rye*. J.D. Salinger. Little Brown Books. 1991. Page 99.
4. *A Separate Peace*. John Knowles. Simon and Schuster. 2003. Page 48.
5. *Flight*. Paramount Pictures. 2012.

6. *Catcher in the Rye.* J.D. Salinger. Little Brown Books. 1991. Page 173.
7. 2 Corinthians 8-11. Page 1796.
8. "George Washington Quote" https://thefederalistpapers.org/founders/washington/george-washington-quote-spark-of-celestial-fire-called-conscience 3-25-2019.
9. Robert E. Lee Quotes. http://www.americancivilwarstory.com/robert-e-lee-quotes.html 3-25-2019.
10. *The Road to Character.* David Brooks. Random House. 2016. Page 211.
11. *A River Runs Through It.* Norman McClean. The University of Chicago Press. page 81.
12. "Quotes Falsely Attributed to Winston Churchill." https://winstonchurchill.org/resources/quotes/quotes-falsely-attributed/ 3-25-2019.

Chapter 7

1. *Counterfeit Gods.* Tim Keller. Penguin 2011.
2. *Flowers for Algernon.* Daniel Keyes. Mariner Books. Page 16.
3. *Flowers for Algernon.* Daniel Keyes. Mariner Books. Page 17.
4. *Flowers for Algernon.* Daniel Keyes. Mariner Books. Page 28.
5. *Counterfeit Gods.* Tim Keller. Penguin 2011.
6. *The Formative Years.* William Pressly.

Chapter 8

1. *Madison Park: A Place of Hope.* Eric Motley. Zondervan. 2017. Page 199.
2. James 1:2-4. Page 1881.
3. https://www.youtube.com/watch?v=LR6PV-Irv7s "Natalie Merchant - Kind and Generous (w/intro) (VH1 Live, 2005). January 16th, 2016. Retrieved January 27th, 2020.
4. *To Kill a Mockingbird.* Harper Lee. Perennial. 2002. Page 241.

Chapter 9

1. Hebrews 12: 3-14. Page 1877.
2. Matthew 7: 1-5. Page 1505.
3. Micah 6:8b. Page 1447.
4. Proverbs 27:17. Page 1024.
5. R.E. Lee: Biography. http://penelope.uchicago.edu/Thayer/E/Gazetteer/People/Robert_E_Lee/FREREL/4/28*.html 3-25-2019.

Conclusion

1. "Everything's Going to be Alright." Kenny Chesney and David Lee Murphy. https://genius.com/David-lee-murphy-everythings-gonna-be-alright-lyrics 3-25-2019.

From the Pages of *When I See It*

"Laughter dampens our woes in a way that it not only stops the pain, but gives a chance to learn from it, thus enabling us to be stronger the next time."

– CHAPTER 2

"Shift your reason for happiness based on *other's* happiness instead of your *own*, and you will be more fulfilled; I guarantee it."

– CHAPTER 2

"When you're given something, you've got to pass it... pass it on, pass it around, or pass it backwards. Not to do so is not only unappreciative, but also an insult to God."

– CHAPTER 2

"When I look at the happiest of people, they are most happy when another succeeds, not themselves."

– CHAPTER 2

"It's not just that when one door closes, another opens, often times you'll that when your door opens, you'll get to have the opportunity to open that same door for others— creating an environment that never could have happened if that originally door hadn't closed. Having a door closed only means God is going to present you with an opportunity to open more doors for others—and Him—in the future."

– CHAPTER 3

"We are often fearful of what we don't know because fear is often born out of ignorance; the worst part of this is that it can lead to quick judgment—most the time that judgment being wrong."

– CHAPTER 3

"How is it that we fail to see people for who they really are more often than not? Is it pride, is it pain? Or insecurity? As human beings, we are all so different, but nonetheless so similar in the fact that we often succumb to the mistake of rushing judgment on one another, and even if we don't rush that judgment, we often make the mistake of judging one another on inconsequential aspects of our life instead of things that matter."

– CHAPTER 3

"Compromising yourself is easy in times of trouble, but ultimately, there's always only one side that's right in disagreement, and that side is truth; to live the truth might mean sacrificing something, but in sacrificing that something, you'll find that you gain true honor and dignity—which could have never come without the sacrifice."

– CHAPTER 3

"The cover—or the outside —distracts us from seeing what's on the inside more often than not even though it contains no content—or, nothing to learn from. When people refer to what percentage of a book they've read, they often describe their progress in the number of pages read. They're telling you how much content they have gotten through; only then can they truly judge a book. Judge people in the same way. Count the pages you've read before you start drawing conclusions."

– CHAPTER 3

"Layers in a cake can be challenging to read because if you look from the top down, you can't see that there are even layers in the first place; it just seems like there is one consistency in whatever it is you're looking at. But it you see the cake at eye level, you'll soon see a cake for what it's really worth—the whole picture. To see the whole picture, you must be at eye-level, meaning that you're willing to look at the cake in the same way it glances back at you. In the same way, humans must look at each other in the eye; they must make eye contact. Only then can you see the other person in their true light."

– CHAPTER 3

"Walking with God also means that you are willing to take a risk; sometimes that risk may involve you may look like a complete fool to others. If that's the case don't sweat it, for a fool to humans is often just the person God uses most to carry out His will."

– CHAPTER 4

"It's interesting for me to look back on my own life and realize what has happened because certain things didn't happen. It reiterates to me that God had a plan for my life, and He knows not only how to shape it but direct it."

– CHAPTER 4

"When we hesitate, we are telling the thing or someone that we want that we don't want them—that they're not important in our life. When we have a chance to do God's will and don't act on it, we are telling Him that he is not the number one priority in our life. This disappoints God more than anything, because ultimately, he knows what's best for us."

– CHAPTER 4

"It was time to go into the world and see where I could leave my mark. My depression had ended now that I had finally seen some light, but what was I to do with my light? When you're an occasional runner, tying your shoes to go out and run is the hardest part; for me, it was time to tie my shoes. Learning how to tie one's shoes is something we learn how to do as a child, but the more and more we live, often times, the more and more we forget how to do this simple act. We're scared of what might happen if we fail; or, are we more afraid of what will happen if we succeed? Whatever it is, tying one's shoes is difficult, but with the Lord's help—and with His purpose in mind—we can do it each and every day."

— CHAPTER 4

"I've learned that the outside is here today and gone tomorrow, but the inside of each one of us is what really counts, for the inside is what creates our outward actions which affect other's insides."

— CHAPTER 4

"It's difficult to realize that God is in control, but when we do, we have a better avenue to live out His will because deep down we always know that He wants what's best for us. During the moment this type of thinking can be challenging to say the least. People often say that patience is a virtue; what it is as well is a test—a test of your faith in God."

— CHAPTER 5

"It's difficult to realize that God is in control, but when we do, we have a better avenue to live out His will because deep down we always know that He wants what's best for us. During the moment this type of thinking can be challenging to say the least. People often say that patience is a virtue; what it is as well is a test—a test of your faith in God."

— CHAPTER 5

"For me personally, along with my many other flaws, I admit that I might be one of the most impatient people on the planet. Atlanta traffic drives me crazy, slow play on the golf course ahead of me is irksome, but most of all, when I want something in my life to happen and God doesn't provide it right then and there, I'm frustrated; I think He doesn't get it. Little do I know, that God does get— much better than I do, in fact."

— CHAPTER 5

"It reminds me of us shooing away God in our own lives; we can tell God to go away all we want, but He has this unfathomable ability to always watch over us even when we tell him to go away. Having God in your life is like getting super glue on your hands; He—or it—can just never seem to go away. When we cling to God, he holds on even tighter to show us we are firmly in His grasp."

– CHAPTER 5

"Entrepreneurs who make a lot of money are so successful because they are able to think outside of the box. Thinking outside the box means the perimeter is going to bigger than simply thinking inside the box. It's a risk, and it ultimately takes more effort, but in the end, it's the only way to achieve success. When you think outside the box, and don't judge a book by its cover, paradoxically, you are able to within a person; you're able to see them for who they truly are."

– CHAPTER 7

"Beauty is found from within because our actions are ultimately the only thing we have control over. That's the gift of free-will. The cross is the most important thing in Christianity, but once your sins are atoned for, God doesn't want you just to pray all day and sing and thank Him for it, he wants you to be a man after His own heart and spread the Gospel. He wants you to do all these things in response to that great gift you were given."

– CHAPTER 7

"It's interesting how unselfishness acts often pay dividends for us in the future; it's almost as if God sees where our heart is, appreciates it, and rewards us for our self-denial."

– CHAPTER 6

"In the same vein, it's an interesting point to wander why God made us in the first place. An answer you might normally get to that question is that He was lonely; but that isn't it. Since God is all powerful, omnipotent, and perfect, he doesn't *need* anything. It's the same choice married parents make when they decide to have children: they do so out of love—an unselfish love that transcends all understanding. Not only did our God come down from heaven to atone for our sins, but he also created us in the first place and allows us to have a relationship with Him."

— CHAPTER 6

"A day spent without encouraging others is a day wasted; people need you to be that agent of God in their life; there is no greater impact on your life than to impact others."

— CHAPTER 6

"In order to start a relationship—whether it be romantic or simply friendship—there has to be a sense of permanence that will always be there. Without that, relationships cannot form properly—or at all."

— CHAPTER 6

"Jesus wants us to dream like we used to dream when we were children. Only when we do so will we accomplish the will of the Father in heaven. Early on in our childhood, all of us had dreams; many of us when we grow older, forget them. We forget them because we lose our childlike faith that *anything* can happen with God. We start listening to the naysayers, we start to let the harsh world bring us down, but most of all, we become pessimistic and then start to believe, that even with God's help, the unthinkable can't happen. That's why we need children around us; that's why we need to become *like* children."

— CHAPTER 6

"In many ways, it is how God appears to us. We can only see Him when we need Him the most. We have free-will, but he is still guiding our steps. We should know that God is always within ear shot, even if we are miles from Him on a rainy today. He said he would be with us—always. The word always has a sense of permanence that no other word in the English language has. It's both final and complete."

— CHAPTER 7

"The cross is the most important thing in Christianity, but once your sins are atoned for, God doesn't want you just to pray all day and sing and thank Him for it, he wants you to be a man after His own heart and spread the Gospel. He wants you to do all these things in response to that great gift you were given."

— CHAPTER 8

"To truly empathize with someone, more often than not means that you want them to have a *different* outcome. You want things to change for the better for them. And you want to be part of that avenue for change."

— CHAPTER 8